Team-Building Activities
for the
Digital Age

Team-Building Activities
for the
Digital Age

Using Technology to Develop Effective Groups

Brent D. Wolfe
Colbey Penton Sparkman

Human Kinetics

Library of Congress Cataloging-in-Publication Data

Wolfe, Brent D., 1973-
    Team-building activities for the digital age: using technology to develop effective groups / Brent D. Wolfe, Colbey Penton Sparkman.
        p. cm.
    Includes bibliographical references.
    ISBN-13: 978-0-7360-7992-1 (soft cover)
    ISBN-10: 0-7360-7992-0 (soft cover)
    1. Team learning approach in education. 2. Internet in education. I. Sparkman, Colbey Penton, 1972- II. Title.
    LB1032.W66 2010
    373.13'60785467--dc22

                                    2009029429

ISBN-10: 0-7360-7992-0 (soft cover)
ISBN-13: 978-0-7360-7992-1 (soft cover)

The Web addresses cited in this text were current as of October 2009, unless otherwise noted.

Acquisitions Editor: Gayle Kassing, PhD; **Developmental Editor:** Ray Vallese; **Assistant Editor:** Derek Campbell; **Copyeditor:** Tom Tiller; **Permission Manager:** Dalene Reeder; **Graphic Designer:** Joe Buck; **Graphic Artist:** Patrick Sandberg; **Cover Designer:** Keith Blomberg; **Photographer (cover):** Keith Blomberg; **Photographer (interior):** Courtesy of the authors, unless otherwise noted; **Photo Asset Manager:** Laura Fitch; **Visual Production Assistant:** Joyce Brumfield; **Photo Production Manager:** Jason Allen; **Printer:** Versa Press

Printed in the United States of America   10   9   8   7   6   5   4   3   2

The paper in this book is certified under a sustainable forestry program.

Human Kinetics
Web site: www.HumanKinetics.com

United States: Human Kinetics
P.O. Box 5076
Champaign, IL 61825-5076
800-747-4457
e-mail: humank@hkusa.com

Canada: Human Kinetics
475 Devonshire Road Unit 100
Windsor, ON N8Y 2L5
800-465-7301 (in Canada only)
e-mail: info@hkcanada.com

Europe: Human Kinetics
107 Bradford Road
Stanningley
Leeds LS28 6AT, United Kingdom
+44 (0) 113 255 5665
e-mail: hk@hkeurope.com

Australia: Human Kinetics
57A Price Avenue
Lower Mitcham, South Australia 5062
08 8372 0999
e-mail: info@hkaustralia.com

New Zealand: Human Kinetics
P.O. Box 80
Torrens Park, South Australia 5062
0800 222 062
e-mail: info@hknewzealand.com

E4705

To those tireless educators who believe that students learn best when the lessons are personal and action oriented, this is for you.

—Brent D. Wolfe

This book is dedicated to all of the great college students I have been honored to journey with during my tenure as a collegiate minister and to my fellow collegiate and campus ministers who serve students daily by helping them grow in their understanding of God and of the world in which they are called to love and serve.

—Colbey Penton Sparkman

Contents

Activity Finder

Activity	Category	Focus	Page
All Roads Lead to Here	Audio and video	Different paths	180
ASCII Art	Internet	Perspective	113
Behind the Seen	Internet	Historical and current events awareness	72
Blog About It	Internet	Honest sharing and reliability and credibility of information found on the Internet (other focuses depend on blog topic)	91
Bumper Sticker Philosophy	Photo	Self-expression	55
Caption Action	Photo	Different perspectives	59
Crossing the Line	Internet	Similarities and differences	96
DbT (Death by Text)	Texting	Observation and memory	127
Emotional Expressions	Photo	Identifying emotions	63
E-terpretations	Internet	Interpreting meaning	79
Everyone's a Critic	Audio and video	Cultural sensitivity and group consensus	175
The Eyes Have It	Photo	Different perspectives	50
Fact or Fiction	Internet	Discernment	93
Family History Collage	Photo	Interconnectedness and community	61
First Impressions	Audio and video	Stereotypes	177
Following the Leader	Texting	Leading and following	152
Forward Legends	Internet	Discernment	99
Freeze-Frame	Photo	Attention to detail	65
Get an Earful	Internet	Self-exposure	109
Got a Song for It!	Audio and video	Teamwork and problem solving	163
Hardware Hunt	Texting	Reciprocity	138

(continued)

Activity Finder *(continued)*

Preface

*T*eam-Building Activities for the Digital Age is the first series of team-building activities to creatively engage young adults living in an age of cyber communities. Offering more than 50 activities designed to strengthen young people's communication through use of the cutting-edge technology they thrive upon, this book helps readers build genuine, face-to-face connections. Understanding the importance that young adults place on self-expression—as evidenced in everything from their tattoos and personalized ringtones to their use of social networking sites such as Facebook and MySpace—our goal is to encourage students and young adults to positively express their individuality and uniqueness to others. In a fresh approach to team building, *Team-Building Activities for the Digital Age* introduces brand-new activities and adds technological twists to proven methods. While technology changes rapidly, the lessons taught through these activities will last and help groups become more effective.

In testing various activities, and in our regular conversations with other professionals and students, we decided that using this generation's technology is essential to reinforcing the lessons we hope to teach. It takes only a quick glance around any high school or college campus to see that a large percentage of students are either talking or texting on a cell phone or listening to music as they move from class to class. Because this book was designed with these individuals in mind, we found it essential to use technology in which they are well versed, even if the technological requirements occasionally make the activities a little more challenging to implement than is the case with more conventional team-building activities.

Identifying the Target Audience

The intended participants for this guide's activities are referred to variously by means of terms including *digital natives*, *Generation Y*, *echo boomers*, the *Millennium Generation*, *MyPods*, *baby boomlet*, and the *Boomerang Generation*. Regardless of terminology, they include a group of young adults born anywhere from the late 1970s through the early 2000s (Shapira 2008). As that range of years suggests, this generation, in addition to being difficult to label, is also difficult to define in terms of dates, and considerable discussion has been devoted to narrowing down the composition of Generation Y. Most authors agree, however, that the outer reaches of the relevant time frame are marked by the late 1970s and early 2000s.

In *Grown Up Digital: How the Net Generation Is Changing Your World*, Don Tapscott (2008) posits eight norms that help define this particular generation:

- Desire for freedom in all situations and experiences
- Opportunity to customize and personalize
- Ability to scrutinize and question
- Desire for integrity and openness in work environments
- Tendency to combine entertainment and play with work and education
- Emphasis on collaboration and relationships
- Speed in accessing information
- Having the opportunity to innovate

Members of Generation Y tend to seek flexibility and acceptance of their preferences, and they are not willing to sacrifice these desires. In a 2009 issue of *Computerworld*, Cindy Waxer interviewed baby boomers and members of Generation Y as she sought to gain deeper understanding of the latter group. According to one interviewee, "Millennials [i.e., members of Generation Y] really want a work-life balance that's seamless; they want to be able to communicate with their friends while they're working." This enmeshing of work and the rest of life mirrors several of the norms suggested by Tapscott (2008) and serves as a reminder that Generation Y is different from past generations and thus the way we work with these individuals should also be different. In the same article, Waxer suggested that "Businesses that expect all employees to march to the beat of the same drummer . . . may have a tough time reining in millennials' more spirited work ethic and thirst for experimentation." This kind of change requires a response from those who are educating the members of Generation Y; whether we are high school teachers, youth pastors, college professors, or members of residence life or university orientation staffs, the way we teach Generation Y must be revamped. In an article titled "Listen to the Natives," Marc Prensky (the author who coined the term *digital natives*) warned that "educators have slid into the 21st century—and into the digital age—still doing a great many things the old way. It's time for education leaders to raise their heads above the daily grind and observe the new landscape that's emerging" (2005–2006). It is in answer to this call to serve today's digital youth in a thoughtful manner that we offer the activities in this book, which are designed to meet young adults where they live and use methodologies with which they are comfortable.

A recent study of the influence and spread of technology among 7,700 college students offered some telling statistics related to this generation's use of technology (Junco and Mastrodicasa 2007):

- 97 percent owned a computer.
- 76 percent used instant messaging (IM), and 15 percent of IM users were literally connected 24-7.
- 95 percent owned a cell phone.
- 28 percent owned a blog, and 44 percent read blogs.
- 34 percent used Web sites as their primary source of news.
- 49 percent downloaded music from the Web.
- 75 percent had a Facebook account.
- 60 percent owned a portable music or video device.

Clearly, then, this generation is using technology extensively. The fact that 97 percent of college students own a computer is telling enough in itself, and the picture becomes even sharper when one examines what the students are doing with their computers. This generation uses technology for communicating, for developing and maintaining friendships (e.g., through instant messaging, Facebook, blogs), for learning about current events (through blogs and Web sites that serve as primary sources of information), and for entertainment (by downloading and listening to music electronically). Never before has technology been so readily available—or so heavily used in the ways in which this generation is using it.

Our book seeks to meet the members of this generation where they live by using their technology in ways that they are familiar with and adding subtle twists to provide opportunity for education and enlightenment.

Using This Book

Team-Building Activities for the Digital Age is divided into several sections. Chapter 1 ("Operating System") serves as a how-to or user's guide for the book as a whole. It opens with a discussion of practical techniques for planning, preparing, and leading the book's activities. Next, the chapter offers multiple suggestions related to safety; providing a safe physical and emotional environment is crucial for success in any team-building experience. The final section of the chapter offers suggestions for making activities not only fun and exciting for participants but also significant and engaging on a deeper level. Our research on Generation Y supports the notion that these individuals don't just want to have fun; they also seek compelling experiences and want to create greater meaning in their lives.

The remaining chapters focus on relationship-building activities that use several types of popular technology. To help you with planning, the chapters are organized on the basis of certain technologies; you'll find activities that involve digital photos, digital videos, the Internet, texting, cell phones, and MP3 players.

We have streamlined the activities listed in each chapter by using a consistent structure for discussing them. Each activity discussion includes the following sections:

- Overview: Describes the activity in a nutshell.
- Directions: Explains what group members are supposed to do.
- Focus: Offers our suggested goal for the activity.
- Equipment: Lists technology and other materials needed for the activity. We also discuss how many units are needed for each type of equipment (e.g., cell phone for each user). For activities that require specific preparation, we provide guidance for completing the preparation phase.
- Users: Lists the number of participants and, where needed, specifies the number of groups they should form.
- Processing: Expands participants' opportunities to learn from their experience by offering several questions to jump-start conversation and help participants apply the activity to their own lives.

- Go Wireless!: Provides suggestions for completing the activity without technology.
- Upgrade: Discusses optional methods for modifying the activity or making it more challenging.

Stressing Safety

Whenever individuals interact in a group, there is a risk of injury, whether physical or emotional. Although the potential for physical injury while participating in these activities is minimal, we encourage every reader to plan the activities carefully and ensure that group members are completely comfortable with any physical safety issues that may arise. For example, when asking participants to take pictures of bumper stickers as they will in Bumper Sticker Philosophy, make sure to remind students to be alert for cars as they will be walking in parking lots. As for emotional safety, which is sometimes taken for granted, we want to offer words of both encouragement and caution. In order for relationships to develop, participants must engage in some level of self-disclosure, which opens up the possibility of emotional injury. Thus it is paramount when facilitating these activities that you establish a safe atmosphere in which participants feel free to share honestly and thoughtfully. We recommend that, prior to each activity, you establish some form of a group contract whereby all group members agree to support and listen to one another, share honestly, respect each other's opinions, agree to disagree where necessary, listen before speaking, and pledge not to share revealed information with others outside the group. If participants support alternative viewpoints and gently encourage each other throughout the activities, they will create the best possible opportunities for developing relationships and for growing—both as a group and as individuals. These ideas, along with other safety concepts, are addressed in more detail in chapter 1.

Citing Sources

Our intent has been to create or adapt activities in such a way that they involve current technology. In some cases, we have developed activities from scratch; in others, we have adapted existing activities to incorporate current technology. One of the inherent difficulties in presenting such activities lies in giving credit to the originator (indeed, for activities that have been modified over a long period of time, identifying the original creator can be almost impossible). However, we have made good-faith efforts to locate the developers of activities that are not original and provide credit to their creators. In an effort to give credit where it is due, we also include a bibliographic reference for the activities that are not new or substantially different from the originals. By no means do we intend to claim others' work as our own; we have simply attempted to offer a unique twist that might better reach today's students.

Reaching Students

We believe that reaching students where they live is a top priority in both the educational and relational realms, and we have designed this book specifically with that ideal in mind. We hope that the fun and unique activities outlined in this text will help your students forge improved relationships.

Acknowledgments

This book would not have been possible without the support of my wife, Becky. She stood with me every step of the way and encouraged me when the words and ideas seemed to dry up. She knew this was possible long before I did. I love you, Beck! Thank you too, Austyn Grace! You provided me with inspiration, and I hope that when you are older you will participate in some of these activities. I must also acknowledge the support and encouragement from my parents, Dave and Flo, and my "little" brother, Bryan. You all have inspired me and I thank you for everything.

Thank you to all of my students at Georgia Southern University. You all tolerated my crazy ideas and allowed me to use you as guinea pigs to test many of the ideas in this book. Thank you especially to Kelly, Audrey, Christy, Whitney F., Alexia, Eric, Kelsey, Dustin, Susanna, TeErika, Meaghan, David, Whitney M., Jaden, Jessica, Randy, T.J., Katlyn, Miranda, and Jordan. You all provided some excellent suggestions on how to improve the activities in this book.

Finally, I would be remiss if I did not acknowledge the following two people. First, my co-author Colbey has been excellent to work with! She is one of the most creative people that I know, and she constantly amazed me with her unique and creative ideas. Second, thank you to Mabel. You guided me to the career that I am in and you believed in me. I am deeply indebted to you and your guidance during my undergraduate years.

—Brent D. Wolfe

First, I want to thank my amazing husband, Larry. Without your encouragement, the dream of this book would never have become a reality. Thank you for insisting that Brent and I meet. Thank you for encouraging my dreams and believing in me. I also need to thank our three preschool girls—Emori, Aubri, and Kennedi—for patiently waiting for your mama to color with you, pour your drink, and so on, while I typed away at the computer.

Melissa Cirino, thank you for helping me brainstorm ideas for activities, forming the idea for the T9 Twist activity, and just being excited about this project. Jamie Roberts, a wonderful friend, thanks for giving of your time and incredible editing skills to help us form the proposal for and the content of this book. Sharon Miles, thanks for being a great friend and partner in ministry. Aaron, Eli, Daniel, Smiley, Jennifer, Taylor, and Josh, thanks for taking time out of your day to test activities with me and serve as beautiful models.

And last, but certainly not least, thank you to our editors at Human Kinetics. Gayle Kassing, thanks for believing in our book. Ray Vallese, thank you for being patient with us and helping us make this book better.

—Colbey Penton Sparkman

Operating System

I n this cyber age, members of groups sometimes need opportunities to build a real sense of community and learn to communicate with one another face to face. The activities in this book can be a great place to start. They help groups grow by helping members get to know and appreciate each other's similarities and differences, engaging participants in topics and issues relevant to the group, and encouraging individual contributions. First, though, let's look at some tips for implementing effective team-building activities. The suggestions offered in this chapter, while specific to the activities provided in this book, can be adapted to any type of team-building activity.

Five Things a Facilitator Should Know

Even though a given activity is intended as a tool for building community, it can quickly turn into a disaster that leaves group members wanting to withdraw from the process. When the facilitator is not properly prepared, or does not believe in the process, participants will sense it. Thus, in order for growth activities to be successful, you as the facilitator should know your purpose, your audience, your environment, the needed equipment and supplies, and when to change plans to adapt to the participants.

Know Your Purpose

While the overall purpose of all of these activities is to improve team-work within your group, it is vital to select specific focuses to aid in the process. By clearly defining the purpose of an activity, you increase the likelihood that your group will begin to function more effectively and cohesively. Do you want the people in your group to learn each other's names? Do you want them to learn how to think creatively? Do you want to introduce a specific topic for discussion? Choosing a specific purpose for an activity gives you and the participants more respect for the process and increases the likelihood that the group will become more cohesive because there is a clearly targeted purpose to the activity. Thus each activity presented in this book hinges on a clearly defined purpose to help you target specific areas that your group needs to address.

Know Your Audience

Will the participants include a lot of new people, or do they generally know each other already? When a group includes new people, it is best to select activities that allow participants to get to know one another. Activities such as Ringtone Relay, A Picture Is Worth a Thousand Words, and What's on Your Playlist? offer great ways to help new groups break the ice. On the other hand, groups where members know each other's names and are familiar with each other's tendencies in various situations might benefit more from activities such as Y3W, Self-Portraits, or Mirror, Mirror, on the Wall because these activities require a greater depth of knowledge about group members and increased self-disclosure.

One of the unique aspects of the team-building activities described in this book is that they were designed to be as inclusive as possible. Rather than ask group members to swing on ropes, lift objects, or climb to the top of objects, the activities mostly call for participants to think together and collectively solve problems or create solutions. If you have group members with physical disabilities, ask them how you can help them be involved; for most of these activities, a quick conversation on the topic is all you need in order to promote optimal participation. Remember, the point is to help people feel included—like they belong.

Know Your Environment

Several important questions arise here. Will you have enough space for the activity? For example, if an activity requires a large open area, make sure that there is adequate space for people to move around (e.g., without bumping into chairs or people). Also, how long will the activity take? Make sure it will fit into the time period you have available. Does the activity work best for a large group or a small group? We do not list a maximum size for the activities discussed in this book; rather, we suggest that your group be split into smaller groups ranging from 2 to 5 members each. Understanding your group's needs, as well as the suggested group sizes, will help you determine the best location for a given activity.

Know What Supplies You Need

We all have technology-related horror stories to share. Whether it was the big presentation that didn't work because of the wrong version of Microsoft® Office® or the vital e-mail that went nowhere due to a faulty Internet connection, we have all had our struggles with technology. As a result, we cannot overemphasize the importance of making sure that you have the necessary equipment and that it is all working correctly. Make sure that you have everything before the activity begins. Are the camera batteries charged? Is the Internet connection working properly? Do you have all the cords for the LCD projector? For example, if you are going to do Ringtone Relay and are working with a large group, make sure that the microphone is working properly and can pick up a cell phone's ringtone. Each activity in this book includes a list of supplies, but it falls to you as facilitator to make sure that all equipment is working properly *before* you need to use it.

Know When to Change Your Plans

Watch your participants. If they are not having fun or don't seem to be learning the intended lesson, then it is time to break up the activity and move on to something else. The fact that an activity didn't work does not mean that you can't try it again later. If an activity doesn't seem to work well, ask the participants—at a later time—what made the activity difficult and what might have made it better. Addressing any concerns during an activity can take away from the flow, and any concerns regarding specifics about the activity or the manner in which it was facilitated would be best shared at a later time. The activities presented in this book are diverse, and some will work better than others with any given group. Your task as facilitator is to determine which ones are right for each group you work with. Just don't give up! Keep talking with each group and keep trying new activities to help group members learn how to work together.

Importance of Team Building

The term *team building* is heard so often that it is easy to forget what it really means. The idea is to build a team, and this is ultimately what the activities in this book are designed to do—help *build* your team. One doesn't have to look very far to find examples of both successful and unsuccessful teams. Our premise for this book is that in order to build a team, you must build the relationships within that team. Admittedly, some successful teams have involved relationships that were fundamentally flawed—for example, the NBA champion Los Angeles Lakers during the early 2000s, when Kobe Bryant and Shaquille O'Neal continually jockeyed for the status of top star on the team—but for many teams such personality conflicts and relationship difficulties are disastrous. Every activity presented in this book requires constant interaction between participants, and we believe that it is through this interaction that relationships are developed and teams are built.

This approach is supported by contact theory, which suggests that "changes in attitude depend primarily on the condition under which contact occurs" (Allport 1954, cited in Devine and Dattilo 2000, 143). According to contact theory, if the context for contact (i.e., experience in which participants meet and interact) is positive, then their attitudes toward one another are likely to be positive as well. It is the facilitator's challenge to create such an environment, and we discuss this point in great detail later in this chapter. Contact theory also suggests that, aside from context, contact that is positive in itself is likely to create positive attitudes among group members toward each other (Allport 1954). This idea informs our goal for the team-building activities presented in this book—to create positive experiences in order to create positive relationships that, in turn, create positive teams. Tripp, French, and Sherill (1995) suggested that *un*favorable experiences within a group are likely to lead to competition, unpleasant feelings, and frustration. Favorable experiences, on the other hand, lead to productivity, common goals, and relationships that last. This is an excellent argument for building a team. The more individuals connect, the more they find similarities, and the more they are able to work together, the more successful the team will be.

To build your team, it is important for your participants to be engaged with one another, and they cannot engage if they don't know each other. This point may seem overly simple, but we have found that it is over-looked in many settings. Team leaders and facilitators often search for that magic trick—that one technique or idea that will help their group jell. In reality, of course, there is no magic trick; there is, however, a good starting point for your journey in building your team, and that point is engagement. Engage your group. Get to know your group. Make sure that your group members know each other.

Both of us have worked with thousands of adolescents and young adults, and we have seen that they don't always engage to the extent that we would like. When functioning in groups, we (i.e., most people) often seem naturally to gravitate toward those who look like us, act like us, think like us, and even talk like us. In short, we tend to hang out with our friends. In teams (especially larger teams), this tendency can be quite damaging to the overall unity of the group. As cliques form from these smaller groups of friends, teams become less able to work effectively because cliques either ignore one another or they remain focused on what is best for their group rather than what is best for the whole group. This is why in almost every activity in this book, we make use of small groups of three or four participants each. We encourage you to create these small groups thoughtfully in order to prevent groups of friends from always getting together. Ideally, each time the large group breaks into smaller groups, the small groups will put totally new combinations of people together. You could always accomplish this by "counting off" in threes or fours, but we have a couple of creative suggestions.

One technique is to hand each person a playing card as he or she comes in the door. Once everyone has arrived, ask all those who have the same card to find each other. For instance, everyone who has a 3 should find everyone else who has a 3. This approach takes some plan-ning to ensure that you have enough cards of the right number so that (a) everyone is in a group and (b) the groups are balanced; at the same time, this approach makes it easy to ensure that there will never be more than four people in a group.

Today's technology makes it easy to socialize without face-to-face communication, but technology also can be an effective tool for team building and group development.

© iStockphoto/Joselito Briones

Another creative method for dividing your group is to hand out images to participants as they come in the door. The underlying approach is the same as with the playing cards; you are just using printed images in this case. For example, you might print three footballs, three basketballs, three softballs, and three golf balls. When it is time to divide into smaller groups, simply ask people to find the others who have the same image.

When using these methods, it is important to make sure that you do not have all of the same card or same image together. Your participants are likely to enter the room with their friends; as a result, if your cards or images are not shuffled, then the friends are likely to end up together, thus defeating the purpose.

A final suggestion for dividing your large group into smaller groups is to encourage everyone to introduce themselves to the members of their small group. We have found that even people who have been in a group together for some time may not be sure of each other's names. Prompting this sharing eliminates awkward moments such as hearing the infamous "Hey you!" or phrases such as "the guy in the red shirt."

As you work to build your team, we encourage you to focus on the specific purposes associated with each activity. Again, in addition to focusing on relationship building, each activity is geared toward a specific purpose that will help your group progress toward forming a cohesive unit. Whenever we are trying to build a team by building relationships, it is possible for an issue that gets raised to tear the team down rather than build it up. The activities presented in this book do require self-disclosure, and they will challenge most people on both the individual and the group levels. Because of this potential for difficulties, we offer this next section on safety.

Virus Protection

Viruses pose one of the greatest threats to a computer's safety. They attack computers on a regular basis, and one of the most effective ways to prevent a loss of information or an identity theft is to maintain up-to-date antivirus software. A different kind of virus comes into play when working with groups of people to help them improve their effectiveness. This kind of virus might involve anything from group members who intentionally sabotage the group's work to uneven ground that causes participants to trip and fall. Whatever the details, such viruses can create safety hazards, wreak havoc, and disrupt your group's growth; thus we want to do everything in our power to limit them. Whenever we lead activities for groups of people, we must be concerned with their safety. Specifically, Bucher and Manning (2005) have identified two types of safety that should be addressed—physical and emotional.

The need for physical safety is obvious; we simply must provide a safe physical environment for our participants. Doing so might involve, for example, reducing the speed at which groups leave a classroom to go and find pictures as they would do in Bumper Sticker Philosophy or offering common sense words of safety about crossing streets. A facilitator should also check the activity location for any objects or conditions that could cause harm to participants; in addition, since many activities discussed in this book take place indoors, it is important that you conduct a safety check in whatever room your group will occupy. For example, when playing Ringtone Relay, participants may want to get up quickly and run to the front of the room, and you should make sure that the space is clear of obstacles that could create tripping hazards. It is also important to use a room that is large enough for the group you are working with so that participants are not stepping on one another as they move around the space.

Some activities even require participation in locations where you cannot be present (e.g., All Roads Lead to Here, First Impressions, and On-Street Reporter). Whenever a group leaves the direct supervision you provide as facilitator, it is crucial that you remind group members of potential environmental hazards they may encounter. In such instances, remind participants to be aware of their surroundings and to proceed safely (e.g., look both ways before crossing streets, keep all group members together).

Overall, however, *Team-Building Activities for the Digital Age* is geared much more toward activities that are primarily cognitive in nature and therefore require relatively little physical movement. As a result, the second type of safety—emotional safety—is crucial. Emotional safety can be compared directly with physical safety; either way, we are talking about protecting our participants' selves—either physically or emotionally—and although emotional safety typically receives less attention than physical safety, it is no less important. Many activities in this book ask participants to reveal something about themselves. They are asked to reflect on themselves and to be honest with themselves and with others in the group, and in order to do so effectively they must feel that they are opening up to one another in a safe emotional environment. In addition to asking participants to reveal things about themselves, some activities presented here are intentionally challenging on an emotional level, and whenever we intentionally place participants in situations where they will be challenged in this way, we must provide means of protection.

Real and Perceived Risks

The activities you read about in this book typically involve two types of risk. The first type—*real risk*—involves risks identified as a result of some technical assessment exploring the likelihood of a possible event. Insurance actuaries, for example, can inform us of the risks involved in many events we face in life and can assign a particular dollar amount to a given event. For the activities presented here, the real risks are minimal. The perceived risks, however, may be much higher, and perceived risks are very real for participants who experience them.

Perceived risk involves an individual's perception of how risky a given activity might be. Thus an activity's perceived risk is not always founded on the real risk that may be involved; nonetheless, because the participant perceives the risk to be very high, it becomes very real to that individual. For example, when participating in The Eyes Have It, there is very little real risk that a person could get injured, and as a result safety might appear to be a relatively minor concern. Consider, however, a participant with skin blemishes around his eyes; for this individual, the perceived risk (i.e., that others might make fun of his skin condition) is very real and can make participation difficult.

Perceived risks are different for every person, and they have the potential to become debilitating. Davis-Berman and Berman (2002) have suggested that perceived risks can be heightened by an individual's experiences (personal or vicarious) and by media presentations. Group members who have had (or know someone who has had) a less-than-positive experience with team-building activities may approach some of the activities in this book with skepticism and even a perception of risk. In addition, team-building activities are not always cast in a positive light in the popular media. Television commercials, for example, often satirize team-building activities in an office environment as unnecessary at best and oftentimes as simply a joke. Similarly, if participants in your group have seen particularly negative treatments of technology in the media or have become cynical about technology, they may experience a perception of risk that can limit or hinder their participation.

As you lead the activities in this book, it is your job not to eliminate perceived risks but to recognize them and help your participants recognize them and work with them. By recognizing that your participants may fear sharing about themselves with the group because of something hurtful in the past, you can help establish a caring environment that encourages safe sharing of information.

One way to provide an emotionally safe environment that limits both real and perceived risk is to use what is called a full value contract (FVC). FVCs originated in adventure-based counseling and have been shown to be effective in creating supportive environments. An FVC provides a list of group rules or guidelines that everyone in the group agrees to abide by for the duration of the activity. The power of an FVC lies in the fact that the group members generate and agree to the selected guidelines. These are not ideas put forth by the facilitator; the group develops them. Of course, as the facilitator, you can offer suggestions, but the group should feel empowered to add, remove, or adapt your suggested FVC content. The more ownership and input the group invests in the FVC, the more effective it will be. Here are some guidelines commonly included in an FVC:

- Respect others and their opinions.
- Agree to disagree.
- What's said here stays here.
- Share honestly.
- Listen before speaking.
- Only one person talks at a time.

The sample contract presented in figure 1.1 is just a suggestion; the most effective FVC will reflect the values of your particular group. We strongly recommend that you create an FVC with your group before beginning any of the activities suggested in this book. Start by explaining the FVC concept to the group, as well as the importance of creating a welcoming and open environment. Then ask group members what values they would like to include in the FVC. Remember that the power of the FVC depends on having participants select the values expressed in it, which means you must be willing to allow the group to develop the values for itself. As participants suggest values, write them down; once the list has been generated, review it and have the group consider whether to make any changes or additions. When the contract has been finalized, type it up and post it prominently so that group members can see their selected values each time they participate in an activity. In addition, we recommend that you review the contract with the group each time you start a new session and whenever new members join the group.

Specific Safety Issues

As you introduce the activities presented here to your group, you might find it useful to consider several specific safety issues: trust, respect, self-disclosure, and interacting with the public.

Trust

Our purpose in writing this book is to provide opportunities for your group to learn how to interact and communicate effectively in a world that is increasingly reliant on technology. For your group to grow in

Full Value Contract

We, the undersigned, agree to follow and abide by the following principles and guidelines:

- Respect one another
- Practice open-mindedness
- Practice timeliness
- Participate fully
- Cooperate with one another
- Experience comfortableness
- Practice patience
- Have fun

_____

Signature

_____

Signature

_____

Signature

_____

Signature

_____

Signature

_____

Signature

_____

Signature

_____

Signature

_____

Signature

_____

Signature

_____

Signature

_____

Signature

_____

Date

Figure 1.1 Sample full value contract.

these ways, participants must develop trust in each other. Without trust, your group is unlikely to experience the full power of these activities. For example, when participating in the Family History Collage activity, it is vital that participants feel comfortable sharing about their home and family life. Participants whose home life and family experiences are not particularly positive will need to feel that they can trust the group as a safe place where they can share honestly.

Respect

It is also important that group members respect each other. It is common in American society these days to see people using sarcasm, often in jest or to get a quick laugh, but even then such comments can lead the targeted person to feel disrespected and thus unsafe when sharing within the group. For example, two activities presented here (In Focus and A Picture Is Worth a Thousand Words) require group members to be creative in offering answers that might be incorrect. If some participants' offerings are deemed insufficiently creative or are consistently met with sarcasm, these group members may tire of serving as the butt of the joke and simply stop sharing their thoughts.

Self-Disclosure

In this day and age, there are almost no boundaries regulating the information that young adults choose to share with others, and it might be a valuable lesson for members of your group to learn that it is sometimes best not to share certain information in group settings. With the advent of Facebook and other social networking sites, more young adults are sharing more and more of themselves without thinking about the consequences. In 2007, a columnist for the *Daily Collegian*, the Penn State student newspaper, was fired because of membership in a certain Facebook group (Go 2007). In March 2009, a Philadelphia Eagles employee was fired for comments that he posted on his Facebook page (Matyszczyk 2009). Whether the consequence involves being fired or being suspended from school because of alcohol-related pictures posted on the Web—as happened to students at Eden Prairie High School in Minnesota ("Eden Prairie" 2008)—it is clear that young adults do not always consider the full ramifications of the Web's inherent lack of privacy.

In creating a safe environment for self-disclosure, you may want to help your group members develop appropriate filters for the information that they share. On the opposite side of the self-disclosure coin, some participants may fear sharing too much information because they are scared of the consequences. Helping group members find the balance between sharing too much and sharing too little involves striking a delicate balance—one that must be found in order to create a safe atmosphere. For example, the activity called Crossing the Line requires participants to share information about themselves and their past. Some of the prompts (e.g., "I am gay or have a close family member or friend who is," "I have been called fat," "I have discriminated against others") require a tremendous amount of self-disclosure, and participants must feel that they are in a safe environment if they are going to share honestly.

Interacting With the Public

Many activities presented in this book involve interviewing, photographing, or making video recordings of people in public places, and you should encourage participants to be as respectful as possible to those with whom they interact. Participants should never capture someone's image without his or her approval. Some of the activities also involve an element of speed (e.g., returning as quickly as possible to the starting location), and participants who perceive this urgency in a way that might

Even when people are separated by physical boundaries, they often place few boundaries on the information they are willing to share with others through technology.

© Brand X Pictures

lead them toward acting rudely toward those they come in contact with should be encouraged to remain calm and polite at all times. Anytime an activity requires interacting with the public, participants should be reminded to respect both the people and the property they encounter. For example, in Our Stranger, group members must attempt to locate someone they do not know and take a picture with that person. As they are attempting to locate the person, they should remain respectful of the public (and, if relevant, of the place of work) and take care to disrupt the natural happenings within the location as little as possible.

Generating Output

The best measure of technology's worth is its usefulness. If it isn't useful—easy to use—it quickly fades into oblivion. The same can be said of many team-building activities; after the experience is over, the lessons are quickly forgotten. Many people have participated in some type of team-building or problem-solving activities (e.g., ropes courses), and one common complaint is that they don't understand why they did the activity. In such cases, participants leave the activity perhaps having been entertained yet remaining unfulfilled. One technique for helping participants understand why they are taking part in an activity is debriefing or processing. We think it is vital to debrief after each activity in order to encourage participants to make personal and group applications from the activities. Debriefing helps your participants leave an activity having been entertained *and* having learned a valuable lesson that they can apply in a future setting.

The activities described in this book are inherently valuable, but simply using them does not in itself enable participants to enjoy all of their potential benefit. These activities were created in the belief that experience alone is not enough. As landmark educational reformer John Dewey (1938) might say, simply providing an experience without placing that experience in context allows for the possibility of miseducation. Therefore, we strongly encourage you not only to use these activities to provide useful experiences for your group but also to help participants learn from their experiences during the activities in a formal way. Toward that end, here are several suggestions for adding a formal education process to each activity presented in this book.

Experiential Learning Cycle

To begin with, it is important to conceive of a process that we would like to work through when we attempt to use experiences and activities to teach lessons. According to the experiential learning cycle put forward by organizational psychologist David Kolb (1984), the process should involve four steps:

- Experiencing
- Reflecting
- Generalizing
- Applying

Experiencing

The experiencing stage is most familiar. This is the time when you use the activities presented in this book to create an experiential education opportunity for those you are leading, and in many cases that is where the process ends: You lead an activity, people seem to enjoy themselves, no one is hurt or injured, and you call it a success. Unfortunately, this approach leaves learning to chance and leaves you unsure of the lessons that your participants are walking away with. It is even possible that participants will leave the activity having learned the exact opposite of what you intended. Consider, for instance, the Ringtone Relay activity, which gives group members the opportunity to identify similarities between their ringtones, which in turn can lead them to identify similarities in musical taste. What if one person doesn't have any of the same music the others have? What if one person has music that others laugh at? It would be possible for such a person to leave this activity feeling more *dis*connected from the group than connected to it. This type of risk is the reason you cannot stop at simply enabling an experience; you must then move into a period of reflection.

Reflecting

During reflection time, participants are encouraged to look back at the activity they just completed and verbalize what they thought and felt, both as individuals and as a group. For this time to be effective, you must help group members establish a sense of comfort and safety with each other. As discussed earlier, one way to do so is through the use of a full value contract (see figure 1.1 on p. 11). During the period of reflection, participants should be encouraged to think about what they just did and take time to mentally relive the experience. In many of the activities described in this book, the large group is divided into smaller groups that work independently. In these cases, the time of reflection should begin with each small group sharing its experience with the larger group. In addition, during any reflection period, all participants should be encouraged to share their reflections, even if they differ from those of others in the group. Making good use of this reflection phase helps participants dig deeper into what they have learned.

Generalizing

During this step, participants should be encouraged to begin thinking about what they have learned through the experience and how they might be able to apply it in their lives. All of the activities presented in this book provide contrived situations that your group is not likely to encounter in the real world; for instance, it is very unlikely that your group will ever be required to act out the songs on their MP3 players. However, the lessons learned in doing the activities (e.g., learning about their "emotional safe place" in the Musical Expressions activity) can be generalized for use in other situations. During this time of generalization, then, your job as facilitator is to help participants recognize similarities between the contrived situation of the activity and situations that they may encounter in real life. This analysis might involve identifying patterns, considering how reactions during the experience mimic reactions in real life, or exploring how what they learned during the experience is similar to or different from personal experiences in real life. At this point, participants should begin to understand the substantive purpose of the activity.

Again, consider Ringtone Relay. The point of this activity is not to see who has the most music on his or her phone or which team can win; rather, the point is to set the stage for talking about self-expression and to encourage participants to understand how they may be viewed by others. If this purpose is unclear, however, the message may be completely lost, but you can use the generalization step to explore the activity's purpose and effectively lay the groundwork for the final step—applying.

Applying

The best evidence that participants have indeed learned something useful is to see them applying it, and this step is the time for participants to put what they have learned into action in ways that are practical and meaningful to them. Because application implies action, this step must nearly always come after the other three stages; that is, participants must have future opportunities to put what they have learned into practice. One way to make this happen quickly is simply to lead multiple related activities from the book during one time period. For instance, during the Bumper Sticker Philosophy activity, participants are asked to talk about issues related to self-expression, which is also the topic of Quotable Quotes, Ringtone Relay, and What Do You See Here? Participating in a second activity involving a certain issue gives participants a chance to immediately apply what they learned in the first activity; for example, while participating in Quotable Quotes, participants could be asked to apply what they learned about self-expression during Bumper Sticker Philosophy.

Regardless of the specifics, asking participants to apply lessons learned during earlier team-building sessions helps them work through the application phase of the experiential learning cycle. In some cases, a larger time gap may be necessary so that participants can individually process what they experienced without the pressure of a facilitator or other group members. In such cases participants should be encouraged to apply the lessons they have learned to situations and experiences in their lives away from the group. Whatever the specifics of your group's situation, you should formally discuss the process of intentionally applying lessons learned to new situations and, where possible, provide opportunities for participants to do so.

The application stage serves two purposes. First, it enables participants to achieve closure as they conclude the process. After participants have had an experience, reflected on it, and drawn generalizations from it, applying what they have learned offers a sense of completion to the activity. Second, application offers opportunity to put what was learned into practice during future experiences both with and without the group. In this way, the four stages are cyclical, and the concluding stage (application) becomes the first stage of a new experience. Thus by

providing opportunities for participants to experience, reflect, generalize, and apply the lesson, you create opportunities for them to learn.

Debriefing Questions

It may be natural at this stage to wonder exactly how, in practical terms,
you can use the four steps just discussed. This is where debriefing
comes into play. This technique enables you to help participants move
from the experience itself into a time of reflection, then into a period of
generalization, and finally into taking action based on what they have
learned. In its simplest form, debriefing simply means asking questions
to highlight behaviors, actions, and comments from participants. The
key to conducting an effective debriefing is to ask questions—lots of
them—but if the debriefing is successful, your voice will not feel tired
at the end, because your participants will have done most of the talking.
During a debriefing, your job is to guide the conversation in a positive
direction and help group members discover the purpose behind the
activity and how they can apply it in their lives. Here are three categories
of questions that you should pose to your group:

- Reliving the experience
- Exploring the purpose
- Applying lessons learned to life

By asking questions in each of these categories, you can help your
participants move from simply having a nice experience to having an
educational experience that can benefit them in future situations. We
provide questions in all three categories for each activity presented in
the book, but we encourage you to use them in conjunction with your
own questions. Be creative in developing questions that make sense to
you and are meaningful to your group. The questions we have provided
are intended as suggestions. While the prospect of posing questions to
your group may seem daunting at first, you will become more comfortable with it as you do it more.

Reliving the Experience

This category of question involves the time of reflection, and questions
should be geared toward helping group members reflect on the experience they have just had. In a very real sense, you want to ask questions
of the group that will help them to, in effect, watch a mental replay of

Physical proximity does not guarantee productive face-to-face communication—not when the participants focus on cell phone chats or Facebook updates.

© Photodisc

what they have just done. During activities such as the ones presented in this book, it is impossible for one person to see and hear everything that goes on, and talking about what happened can help everyone develop a sense of shared context. In addition, some of the activities take a long time, and concerted reflection helps participants remember aspects of the experience that they may have forgotten.

During this time of reliving the experience, you can help participants engage in two levels of reflection: macro and micro. When asking participants to relive the macro experience, you are asking them to relive the entire experience and what they did for the entire time. This is a natural place to begin, and it also leads nicely into the micro level of reliving the experience. At the micro level, your role is to help group members relive a particular experience that occurred during the activity—one instance that was particularly poignant or noticeable. It may have been an argument or an unexpected twist. Regardless of the type of moment, the micro level of reliving the experience is akin to using the pause feature on a video player in order to focus on what occurred at a particular moment.

For each activity presented in the book, we offer debriefing questions in the Processing section of the activity description, and each of these lists begins with questions designed to help group members relive their experience. (Because of the nature of micro-level questioning, it was impossible for us to include any questions of this type in the samples provided for each activity.) In some cases, this process is participant-directed whereby participants simply share their experiences with the larger group; in other cases, the processing is facilitator-directed through a formal question-and-answer period. For all of the activities in the book, we have offered processing questions that you can ask your group; however, several activities (e.g., My Collage, Family History Collage, and Self-Portraits) will also include participant-directed processing. For these activities, participants will begin the processing by sharing information rather than responding to questions provided by the facilitator. We strongly encourage you to spend considerable time helping your group relive the experience, since doing so helps group members understand the purpose of a particular activity.

Exploring the Purpose

By asking questions designed to help group members explore an activity's purpose, we are assuming that there was an intended purpose in the first place. In reality, however, failure to establish a clear purpose is where many activities go wrong. Thus we have clearly identified a purpose for each activity in this book in order to help you plan and prepare for helping your specific group. However, not every activity in the book will be effective for your group; it is crucial that you understand what your group needs. For example, if you want your group to explore differing cultural values, then you would want to select an activity such as Our Values. In contrast, an activity such as Where in the World Am I? would not help the group work on cultural values and thus would likely prove frustrating to all involved.

Know your group, know what your group members need, and select activities that are appropriate for them *where they are*. As you help your group explore the purpose of an activity, you can approach the subject directly by simply asking, "Why do you think we just did this activity?"

or "What was the point of this activity?" Such questions are very effective, but they can become redundant over time. For this reason, in the question lists that accompany each activity, we include questions that will help you explore each activity's purpose with your group by addressing the intended purpose for that specific activity. For example, the activity Who's in Your Phone? is designed to help participants interpret facts from different perspectives, and useful questions to ask might include the following: "How do we interpret information in real life?" "How *should* we interpret information?" "How do you view people who interpret information differently than you do?"

Even though we offer purposes for the activities, you may identify other purposes, and your group may generate still other reasons for participating in an activity. The challenge here is to be grounded yet flexible: Understand why you are leading the selected activity and be prepared to help the group see that purpose, but also be willing to see and explore alternatives presented by your participants. In many cases, participants' insights can greatly expand the range of lessons that can be learned from a given activity.

It has been our experience that as group members explore the purpose of an activity they tend to offer two levels of commentary. The first level is directly related to the activity itself. For example, when exploring the purpose of the In Focus activity, participants may initially state that the purpose was to take close-up pictures of objects so that other teams would have a difficult time guessing what they are. This description is accurate, but it does not get at the activity's deeper purpose; it is concrete and relatively superficial. To go deeper, you may have to help the members of some groups move toward exploring an activity's larger purpose, and in such cases it can be effective simply to ask participants what they have learned. For the In Focus activity, the purpose is to understand perspective and frame of reference. If this is not immediately obvious to participants, you can gently ask questions to help participants move from the concrete to the abstract level of understanding that will help them greatly as they attempt to apply what they have learned.

Applying Lessons Learned to Life

The ultimate goal of a debriefing is to address questions about real-life application of the lessons learned during the activity. If participants have effectively relived their experience, gained understanding of why they engaged in the activity, and identified lessons learned, then they should be prepared to make personal applications in their own lives. The essence of real-life application is transference, and in the debriefing we want participants to consolidate what they have learned and make statements about how they can apply these lessons in real life. In order for questions related to real-life application to be effective, it is important that you have an accurate understanding of your participants' lives. With many groups, this is not terribly difficult because, in working with adolescents and young adults, many facilitators typically gain an understanding of what their participants are experiencing in their lives. This understanding can be as simple as knowing where they work, where they live, where they go to school, and what types of projects they are likely to be involved in. Ultimately, if participants are to apply lessons in their personal lives, the facilitator must help them connect the conversation to experiences that they are likely to have. Thus, for each activity, we provide sample questions related to real-life application, and we have made them as specific as we could without knowing your group. The more specific you can make these questions, the more effective the lessons will be.

During this time of talking about application, it is helpful for you to encourage your participants to be as concrete as possible. You can be more helpful by encouraging them to make "I will . . ." statements than by allowing them to speak in broad generalizations. For example, in the Treasure Hunting activity, one of the application-to-life questions is, "How can we show that we value something—or someone?" If a participant answers by saying, "I can tell someone that I care about him or her," the statement is so broad that it does not readily lend itself to action, which should be the hallmark of answers to this type of question. If you encourage the participant to be more specific, he or she might end up with a statement like the following: "The next time I have a group member who really takes a stand, I will tell her that I appreciate her willingness to stand up for what she believes." This statement frames the point as an action that the participant is committed to taking ("I will . . .") *and* identifies the context in which the person will take the action. The more you encourage participants to apply what they have learned to their personal lives, rather than to their analysis of other people, the more effective the lessons will be because participants will have both an action and a context to demonstrate that action upon completion of the activity.

Remember also that when talking about application, the key is action. When participants are simply asked to answer questions about how they will apply what they have learned, it is easy for them to be overly ambitious in their comments and ideas. One way to avoid this pitfall is to provide time for action by allowing the group to participate in more than one activity during a team-building session. Upon completion of the first activity, tell the group that they are now going to have the opportunity to apply what they have just learned as they participate in a second activity. The debriefing for the second activity could then begin with discussion of how well group members did in applying lessons learned from doing the first activity. An alternative technique for encouraging participants to generate realistic suggestions for application is to use activities presented in this book over the course of multiple sessions. For example, if a group

How do adolescents use technology at home? Facilitators who understand what young participants experience outside the group can help them apply what they learn to their lives.

© Stockdisc Royalty Free Photos

does Self-Portraits during one week's session and the discussion centers on self-awareness, you might follow up on group members' application statements when the group meets for its next session.

Five Debriefing Techniques

In addition to learning about the experiential learning cycle and debriefing question categories, you can also use specific techniques to develop your ability to ask useful questions and help your group learn from the activities presented in this book. Toward that end, here are five techniques to help you in your role as facilitator:

- Questions
- Silence
- Echoes
- Comparisons
- Observations

These techniques are designed to help you during debriefing exercises, but it is important to remember that they form guidelines rather than a recipe that must be followed exactly. You can use them to facilitate conversation among your participants, and we encourage you to develop your own techniques as well.

Questions

One tendency we have noted both in ourselves and in other facilitators is that we like to talk! While this is not a bad thing in itself, it is important when we are acting as facilitators that most of our talking come in the form of questions. At the completion of an activity, you may have some amazing insights that you are eager to share with your group, and it is easy to think that because we are leaders we should go ahead and share what we know. Let us strongly encourage you, however, to temper your desire to offer lengthy insights. Instead, ask questions that help your group members develop their own insights. If participants are allowed to develop their own thoughts and ideas and come to their own conclusions, they are more likely to remember what they have learned. One mark of an effective debriefing session is that you have done nothing but ask questions. As the proverb goes, "Give me a fish and I eat for a day; teach me to fish and I eat for a lifetime." We want to teach our participants how to fish for their own ideas.

You may also find that questions are particularly helpful when you are working with a group whose members are having difficulty completing an activity. Rather than telling a group what to do—how to solve a problem or how to approach a particularly difficult task—ask the participants questions that lead them to develop their own solutions. It is better to gently nudge your group through the use of questions than to simply tell them the answers so that they can move forward. Telling the group the answers does not make them search to find them on their own. We don't want to just give participants the fish. We want them to learn how to fish so that they can continue to use lessons learned in future situations.

Silence

The second technique for helping your group learn is simply to remain quiet, and this can be a difficult task for any leader. After all, in many situations the leader is the person who does most of the talking. As much as is humanly possible, however, we encourage you to limit your talking during and after each of the activities presented in this book. For example, during an activity, you might see a very clear solution or have an insight that would make the group's task much easier. Allow participants to discover it on their own! Even if they don't discover the easy way that you observed, they will still have discovered their own way that works for their specific group. Also, in many cases, your suggestion might make perfect sense to you but not to the group; it might even make the group's task harder. Similarly, during debriefing time, it is important to limit your speaking to simply asking questions. As mentioned earlier, at the end of an activity, your voice should not feel tired; your participants should have done the bulk of the talking.

Echoes

You can also help your group members learn from an activity by reflecting their questions back to them. Throughout these activities, your participants are going to ask you questions—how to complete a task, how to solve a problem, how other groups have done the activity. They may even ask you to complete the task or solve the problem for them. Resist the urge to answer any of these questions! Reflect the question back to your participants and encourage them to develop their own techniques and solutions. For example, during Behind the Seen, participants may ask you whether a particular individual would be good to use. While you could simply answer yes or no, it might be better to ask participants why they think the individual would be a good person to use. In other words, rather than giving them the answer, encourage them to develop their own solutions. This ability to reflect participants' questions back at them improves with practice, but the lessons learned by your group members will be much more influential and long-lasting if participants develop the thoughts, ideas, and solutions for themselves.

Comparisons

You can also encourage participants to create comparisons. Thinking about how their experience during an activity compares with experiences in their personal lives can help them make concrete connections that are more likely than broad generalizations to stick with them. It is particularly effective to use similes and metaphors to help participants connect an activity to their own lives. A simile or metaphor that a participant creates will hold meaning for the group members that will enhance the application of lessons learned.

For example, Mirror, Mirror, on the Wall is a fun activity that allows participants to look at their social networking pages from a new perspective; the true intent of this activity, however, is to allow group members to reflect on their lives. In this case, the metaphor is that one's social networking page serves as a representation of one's life, and different people may look at your page (i.e., your life) and come to different conclusions about what you believe in or stand for.

There are some groups where the use of similes and metaphors are not particularly effective (e.g., groups with younger children or adolescents); in these cases, you can help participants take lessons inward by making more direct comparisons between the staged activity and their lives. For example, the lesson from Mirror, Mirror, on the Wall is much more powerful if participants understand that it involves not just their social networking page but their life as a whole and their personal identity.

Observations

Finally, you may find it helpful to engage in intentional observation during an activity. If we are leading an activity but are not involved in completing it or solving the problem that it poses, we sometimes find it easy to tune out rather than pay close attention to the participants' actions. It is important, however, that group members see that we are invested in the activity, and this means that we may have to train ourselves to pay attention even though we are not directly involved. We encourage you to pay close attention to what your participants say and do during each activity you lead. By engaging in close observation, you not only show your group members that you are involved but also prepare yourself to ask effective questions at the micro level. For example, if you overhear a distinctive comment during the activity, you can ask a question about it during the debriefing time. Through this type of careful observation, you enable yourself to tailor debriefing questions to your group's unique experience and thus greatly increase the chance that participants will learn something truly useful.

Summary

This chapter is designed to provide supporting information to help you make effective use of the activities presented in this book. We have found that team-building activities are most effective when you as the facilitator understand who your participants are, what your want them to learn, and which activities will make this possible. This chapter began with a discussion about what you should know before starting your work with a group. You will be most effective as a facilitator if you know your group's purpose, its members, where you will conduct the activities, what supplies you will need, and when to seek assistance. The chapter also reinforced lessons of safety. It is vital that you use general sensitivity and full value contracts to protect your group members' physical and emotional safety. The chapter concluded by examining the importance of debriefing, as well as specific techniques for facilitating this process. No activity presented in this book should be done without asking the accompanying debriefing questions or the facilitator-designed or -adapted questions. These questions are geared toward the intended purpose of each activity, and you can use them to help your participants consciously recognize the lessons they have learned.

By now, you're ready to start reading, analyzing, and using the activities that make up the rest of this book. We hope that you and your participants enjoy them as much as we have. We have tried to create activities that are meaningful and relevant to today's adolescents and young adults, and our hope is that each activity you use helps your group become more cohesive and effective.

CHAPTER

2

Photo Activities

The ability to take a picture and view it instantly through digital photography has changed the way we communicate and see the world around us. No longer does a person have to take a picture, go to the store, drop off the film, and wait an hour (at best) before picking up the developed pictures. Today, people take pictures on their digital cameras, post them on a social networking site, e-mail them to friends and family, print the images on paper, or upload them to a service that will print them for a fee. As is the case with textual information, pictures are now available immediately. If we don't like an image, we simply delete it or take another one, and we can also receive instant feedback about our images from others. This chapter harnesses the power to view images instantaneously in order to help group members learn more about themselves and how they interact with each other.

The activities presented in this chapter cover a range of focuses that include exploring different perspectives; becoming more self-aware; identifying cultural values; solving problems; identifying roles within a group; exploring methods of self-expression and self-reflection; understanding the importance of diversity and the negative effects of stereotypes; identifying emotions; paying attention to detail; interpreting facts; exploring interconnectedness; and establishing community.

When using digital cameras, the first challenge is to move the images from camera to computer. We recommend three primary ways of doing so: The first method is to use a standard USB cable that connects the camera to the computer. This approach enables you to download images directly from the camera to the computer, and you can then use an LCD projector to allow your group to view the images. The second method is to use a memory card reader (one that is capable of reading different types of memory cards). With this approach, you can remove the memory card from the camera, insert it into the card reader, and download its contents to the computer. The third method is to ask group members to bring the cables that they use at home for downloading their own pictures to their computers. This approach ensures that there is a match for every camera.

For many of the activities presented in this chapter, you will want to create a Web-based photo storage account through a free service such as Flickr or Picasa. In order to use such services, you must have a computer with access to the Internet. It is relatively easy to create accounts on these Web sites, and specific instructions are given at each site. Some of the activities presented here ask group members to use presentation software such as PowerPoint®; as a result, we recommend that you review a given activity thoroughly before attempting to implement it in order to ensure that you have all the necessary technology and that it is working properly.

This chapter contains the following activities:

Who's in Your Phone?

Overview

This activity's purpose is to allow your group to see how information can be interpreted differently from one group to another. Too often, people fall into interpreting information the same way they always have. While this may be acceptable in some situations (e.g., the gas light is on in my car and I interpret that to mean I need gas), in other situations it may be important to have our thinking be flexible to consider alternative interpretations of information. This activity encourages participants to be flexible as they interpret images, thus helping them improve their creative thinking skills. When group members are willing to challenge traditional thought patterns and think "outside the box," the group can be greatly strengthened as they discover new techniques for tackling problems.

Searching individual cell phones for photos from given categories can be a fun way for groups to practice thinking creatively to complete a task.

Who's in Your Phone? *(continued)*

Directions

Prior to the activity, remind participants to bring pictures on their phone or digital camera. To begin the activity itself, have participants form groups of three or four members each, then use an LCD projector to post a list of 15 to 20 picture categories for each group to match with images stored on its members' phones or other electronic devices. For example:

- Athlete
- Baby
- Two people kissing
- Person and pet
- Grandparents
- Something in nature
- Senior school portrait
- Person at the beach
- Person doing something dangerous

Give the groups about 20 minutes to find as many of the requested pictures as possible. Group members can be creative in searching for photos (e.g., search online for a picture), and it is acceptable for a group to take pictures on the spot to fit into a given category. However, do not suggest this idea to the groups; they should be allowed to make interpretations on their own. At the end of the 20 minutes (or earlier, if all groups have finished), state the name of a picture category and ask each group to show its image for that category. Images can be uploaded to a computer and viewed through an LCD projector or simply viewed from each phone or electronic device. For each appropriate image, give the group 1 point.

Focus

Interpreting facts: We tend to interpret what we hear in the manner that is most favorable to ourselves or in the most traditional manner (i.e., the way we've always thought about something). In this activity, participants are asked to interpret a series of facts in a fun and enjoyable way, but a given group's interpretation of those facts may well differ from other groups' interpretations, and the activity's emphasis focuses on the differing standards that the groups use to interpret the facts. For example, if you ask groups to locate a picture of grandparents, many people will automatically try to find a picture of their parents' parents, but the term (as heard rather than as written) can be interpreted in other ways. A group might, for example, locate a picture of parents who are grand (i.e., very good); another option would be to take a picture on the spot of a group member acting as either a grandparent or a grand parent (i.e., a parent who is grand). Such diverse ways of interpreting a seemingly clear-cut term enable the groups to practice thinking creatively.

Equipment
Camera or camera phone for each group, computer, LCD projector

Users
Groups of 3 or 4

Processing
- Which photos were most interesting to you? Why?
- Which pictures were you most surprised to find in a person's phone? Why?
- Which picture would you say was most creatively chosen or created? Why?
- Which picture would you say most accurately fit its category? Why?
- How did your group interpret each of the picture categories? Were there any differences of interpretation within your group on a particular photo?
- Did you bend a picture category or the apparent rules? Did other groups do so?
- How do we interpret information in real life?
- How should we interpret information?
- How do you view people who interpret information differently than you do?
- How should we view people who interpret information differently than we do?

Go Wireless!
Follow the rules for the original version but ask participants to use photos from their wallets or purses. (Again, it is important to advise them to bring pictures with them to the session.)

Upgrade
Have participants produce images for the specified categories by taking pictures of people who are not in their group. While this approach directs the groups in a certain way, it still allows for interpretation of the rules (e.g., what qualifies as an athlete) and it adds an extra level of difficulty as participants must now interact with strangers and creatively interpret the instructions. When using this upgrade, you may want to provide additional time and allow the teams to leave the meeting location as they work to produce the requested images.

Our Stranger

Overview

This activity asks the group to develop problem-solving techniques as they work to locate a stranger. This task may seem impossible at first, but it is doable, and the activity is designed to help participants sharpen their observation skills, improve their problem-solving skills, and begin to identify their roles within the group. The processing questions encourage group members to explore the process they used to solve the problem and articulate their role in that process.

Directions

In preparation for this activity, take pictures of several strangers (you will be asking participants to form small groups, so take a picture of a different stranger for each small group). Be sure to acquire verbal permission from each stranger and clearly explain the nature of the activity; in addition, make sure that he or she will be available when the activity takes place. For example, if the stranger is a person who works at a nearby coffee shop, make sure that the employee gives you permission to include him or her in the activity and that he or she will be behind the counter on the

Tracking down a given stranger helps groups develop their problem-solving skills.

day and at the time of the activity. To maximize your chances of success, we recommend selecting the strangers on the day you are going to have your participants complete this activity.

Begin the activity by having participants form small groups of three or four members each. Explain that the activity is going to be completed in a specific geographic area (e.g., on a college campus) and that they will not have to leave that geographic area (campus) to complete the activity. E-mail or text a picture of each group's stranger to the phone of one group member. Instruct each group to find the person and document how they went about finding him or her. Once a group has found its stranger, the members should take a picture of themselves with the person. Give the groups 30 to 60 minutes to find their assigned stranger—the time limit should be adjusted according to the distance that groups will have to travel and the anticipated difficulty in locating the stranger. Upon returning, the members of each group should share their photos (i.e., the one you provided at the start of the activity and the one they took once they found their person) with the larger group and explain the process they used in their search.

Be sure to include a subtle hint in each picture. For example, if stranger works behind the counter at a nearby coffee shop, you could have a coffee mug in the picture (but *not* with the store logo on it—don't be too obvious). Try to make sure that your strangers are equally recognizable; for example, in working with a group of college students, you would not give one group a picture of a cashier at a grocery store and another group a picture of the university president.

Focus

Problem solving and roles: This activity gives participants a chance to solve a seemingly impossible problem—locating a total stranger. The current generation has multiple mediums at their disposal to solve problems and find solutions. This activity encourages members to think about the plethora of resources to which they have access and explore effective ways of using them. This task may initially strike your participants as very difficult, and it will be vital for them to be resourceful in using their problem-solving abilities to determine how best to approach the job. For example, if the photo includes a coffee mug, participants might start by doing a Web search for coffee shops located nearby. As with any task, people within a group will assume different roles, and in addition to locating their stranger the group members should be encouraged to explore personal roles during their completion of the activity.

Our Stranger (*continued*)

Equipment

Camera or camera phone for each group, photos of strangers

Users

Groups of 3 or 4

Processing

- Did you find your person?
- Who was your person, and where was he or she?
- If you found your person, how were you able to do so—that is, how did you solve the problem posed by this task?
- When you were given the task, what was your immediate thought?
- Did you feel that you had a certain role within the group? If so, what was it?
- If you had a certain role, were you comfortable with it, or did you want a different one?
- How do you typically handle difficult problems when you encounter them?
- Is there any connection between the way you handle difficult problems in your own life and the way you solved the problem posed in this activity?

Go Wireless!

Instead of e-mailing or texting a stranger's picture to each group, you can choose to print the pictures ahead of time and simply hand them out. Then, as in the original version of the activity, tell each group to make sure that someone writes down or remembers the various techniques and methods the group uses to find its assigned stranger. Once all groups return, have each one describe its journey, its assigned stranger, and its overall experience.

Upgrade

Instead of taking pictures, identify a *type* of person for each group to locate (again, a different one for each group)—for example, a woman in charge of a large company, a man who does dirty work, or a child experiencing joy. Provide each group with the description of its category, then instruct the groups to find a person in their category and document how they went about doing so. Each group can find any person they choose so long as he or she fits into the given category. Once a group has found an appropriate person, they should take a picture of themselves with the person.

Encourage the groups to be creative in how they interpret their category descriptions; you might also encourage them to take pictures of several (three to five) people who fit the category. Upon returning, groups should share their photos with each other and explain their search process.

iCaught

Overview

Too many TV shows these days focus on catching people at their worst simply to get a cheap laugh and make fun of the hapless victim. The iCaught activity seeks to use the idea of visually capturing people in a much more positive way. By taking pictures of people engaged in positive actions, participants find themselves exploring a myriad of constructive examples. This activity creates a unique opportunity for your group members to explore issues of interpretation and perspective as they seek instances of positive behavior from the world around them.

Directions

This activity takes place over a period of time—perhaps a week. Ask each group member to take pictures on a specific subject that is important to the group or that is currently being discussed by the group in another setting. For example, you might ask participants to take pictures that represent any of the following: acceptance, beauty, chivalry, choices, courage, forgiveness, freedom, happiness, heartbreak, helplessness, honesty, humility, integrity, leadership, love, mercy, optimism, passion, patience, peace, perseverance, persistence, rescue, sacrifice, service-oriented leadership (i.e., becoming a leader through seeking to serve others), strength, talent, thankfulness, trust, unity. The pictures may be either funny or serious as long as the participant is respectful of the subject. Images might depict people demonstrating a specified quality or suggest the quality in a less concrete fashion. All group members should address the same topic during any given week (this activity can be done many, many times). The pictures can be taken with a cell phone or digital camera.

As participants take images during the week, they should e-mail or text-message their images to you as the facilitator. As you collect the images, insert them into presentation software so that you can show them one at a time during the session. We recommend creating a PowerPoint presentation where each slide contains one picture. When the group comes back together, present the images to the whole group and allow each photographer to take credit for his or her work.

Focus

Interpretation and perspective (other focuses depend on picture topics): The focus of this activity depends greatly on the topic of the pictures; regardless of topic, however, participants will grapple with the issues of interpretation and perspective. Participants must interpret the topic for themselves and determine how they will capture images that are most representative of the topic. We recommend that you give participants a chance to talk not only about the picture topic but also about their thought process behind each picture in order to get them thinking about methods of interpretation.

Equipment

Camera or camera phone for each person, computer with Internet connection, LCD projector

Users

10 to 20

Processing

Processing for this activity begins with having group members identify their pictures.

- What did you learn about the selected topic?
- Which image was the best? How so?
- Which image most accurately represented the topic? How so?
- How did you interpret the instructions?
- Was your interpretation different from others' interpretations?
- Do you feel that anyone's interpretation was wrong? If so, how so?
- How does interpreting the rules for a given situation affect how you make decisions about it?
- Have you ever intentionally misinterpreted a set of instructions for personal benefit or gain?
- How can we learn to correctly interpret directions in the future?

Go Wireless!

Instead of using digital images, ask participants to make mental notes of situations in their experience or observation that are representative of the topic for the week. For example, you could ask participants to note instances of leadership that they saw or experienced during the week. When the group comes together, have participants share their real-life examples with the group.

Upgrade

Many of the topics suggested earlier for this activity are positive in nature and were intentionally selected out of respect for the potential subjects in the images. However, you can take the activity to a different level by asking participants to take images representing qualities or situations that are negative: anger, arrogance, bickering, disappointment, doubt, fear, guilt, ignorance, inequality, jealousy, laziness, manipulation, neglect, peer pressure, pride, regret, revenge, selfishness, stubbornness, vanity, weakness. If you use this version of the activity, you might also introduce a caveat. One possible caveat is that group members may not take pictures of strangers; they must take pictures of people who are in the group that they feel represent the topic. Another possible caveat is that no people be included in the images; that is, participants must take images that show only inanimate objects or elements of nature (including animals). These caveats help protect people who are not part of the group; however, it is still important to protect the people who are in images demonstrating some of these negative behaviors. To do this, we recommend revisiting the full value contract that you established with your group (see figure 1.1 on p. 11). Additionally, remind your group that everyone makes mistakes and that these are just images of people who happened to be exhibiting these behaviors when a camera was on them.

In Focus

Overview

This activity promotes understanding of different perspectives. Participants are asked to examine pictures of objects that are not readily identifiable. As the group attempts to identify the pictured objects, the metaphor of seeing images and life through different eyes remains salient. This activity also asks participants to explore difficulties that may arise when group members are unable to understand different perspectives and thus harmony is elusive.

In Focus *(continued)*

Viewing a smaller part of an object helps groups understand the benefit of each group member's different points of view in seeing the whole picture.

Courtesy of Ross Eli Baylis

Directions

Have participants form groups of three or four members each. Ask each group to take close-up pictures of five to eight objects. Give participants approximately 20 to 30 minutes to leave the room, find their objects, and take their pictures. The decision about whether to remain on-site or have participants venture elsewhere depends on whether your session location offers enough appropriate objects to photograph. In either case, the groups should photograph objects that are difficult to identify in a close-up image—and the more creative the groups are, the more effective the activity will be. Each group should also take full-size images that definitively identify the objects shown in their close-up images.

Though the objects should not be easily identifiable in the close-up pictures, they should be common items that are easily recognizable when seen at full size. For example, the photo above shows a close-up image of the sole of a shoe. Participants could also take a very close-up picture of part of a flower or a recognizable building. Encourage them to be creative and to use different angles and perspectives when they take their close-ups.

Once all of the groups have returned from taking their pictures, download them from their cameras to the computer. Insert all of the images into a presentation software application like PowerPoint and project them onto a screen so that everyone can view them. As an image appears on the screen, each group (except the group that took the picture) should attempt to identify the object out loud. If you want to add an element of competition, you can award each group a point for each correct response. Continue until all pictures have been shown and identified.

Focus

Different perspectives: Sometimes we see very clearly (when we can see the full picture and have a frame of reference); at other times, we can't see very clearly at all (when we are too close to the situation or don't have a frame of reference). This activity encourages group members to think about perspective and how different perspectives can cause conflict or harmony within a group. Although it is unlikely that conflict will arise from this activity, the facilitator can help participants work from the concreteness of the activity toward a useful general truth: When one is too close to an image, or to a certain situation, he or she may have difficulty seeing it clearly and fully, and this difficulty can lead to conflict with others in the group. That is, conflict can arise when people are unwilling or unable to see a problem, task, or activity from another perspective. In contrast, when group members are able to see situations from different perspectives (as participants do when they view images during this activity), they are much more likely to work in harmony.

Equipment

Camera or camera phone for each group, computer, LCD projector

Users

Groups of 3 or 4

Processing

- Which object was most difficult to identify? Why?
- Which object was easiest to identify? Why?
- Did you experience an "Aha!" moment? If so, when, and what led to it?
- How did a change in perspective (from seeing only part of the object to seeing the entire object) lead to a change in your ability to identify the picture?
- What experiences have you had where you were unable to see the whole picture? How have you handled them?
- How can changing your perspective help you handle difficult experiences?
- How has being unable to see the whole picture led to conflict in past situations for you?
- How has seeing the whole picture created harmony in past situations for you?

In Focus *(continued)*

Go Wireless!

Have participants form groups of three or four members each. Ask each group to collect several objects that are relatively obscure (e.g., computer cables, cases for various pieces of equipment, backs of lapel pins, the spring from the inside of a ball-point pen) or that might be unfamiliar when seen out of context (e.g., the case for a Nintendo Wii controller). Once the objects have been collected, each group takes turns holding one of their objects at a time in front of the large group and giving all of the participants an opportunity to identify it.

Upgrade

For anyone who has played Balderdash or a similar game, these adaptations will be familiar. Ask each group to write down a guess identifying each object (whether it is shown in a picture or presented for direct observation); the group that took the picture should contribute a false but plausible answer. The answers are read aloud, and each group then casts a vote for the answer deemed most plausible for a given object. If a group chooses the correct answer, then it earns a point; if a group selects an incorrect answer, then the team that took the picture or chose the object earns a point.

You can also upgrade this activity by having groups take images that are purposefully small and blurry, thus making it even harder for other groups to identify the pictured objects. This activity can serve as a great analogy for situations in which it is hard for a person to perceive the whole picture.

Our Values

Overview

This activity asks participants to engage in considerable interpretation as they articulate what is valued in their culture by taking pictures of objects that they feel represent their culture. Group members are likely to experience anxiety as they struggle to determine the meaning of "our culture" and come to grips with what they believe that culture values through discussing the images collected during the activity.

On a university campus, success in academia is highly valued. As group members take pictures of cultural values, they will gain a better understanding of what others find important.

Directions

Have participants form small groups of three or four members each, then ask the members of each group to go out into the community and take eight pictures that express something that their culture values. The terms *culture* and *value* should be left to each group to define, and the definitions are likely to differ from group to group. Remind the participants that their task is to take pictures *not* of what they personally value but of what their culture values. Each small group's conception of culture might involve any of a number of possible factors. It might, for example, be national, local, or ethnic in nature; it might even involve the small group formed for this activity. However it is defined, each group's notion of culture should be something to which the members feel some meaningful connection. When the groups return to the meeting location, have each group share its photos and explain its rationale for selecting them.

Our Values *(continued)*

Focus

Cultural values: There is value in understanding what is important to individuals within our culture, especially individuals with whom we are teammates. By understanding what is important to other cultures and people from those cultures, we can gain respect and understanding for different ways of living and approaching life. We sometimes disagree with certain values, but critically examining what is valued is extremely important as we try to develop tolerance and understanding of those who we live and are teamed with.

Equipment

Camera or camera phone for each group, computer, LCD projector

Users

Groups of 3 or 4

Processing

Processing for this activity begins with the groups' explanations of their photos.

- Do you hold the same values that your culture holds? Why or why not?
- What do your culture's values say about that culture?
- What do your culture's values say about you as a member of that culture?
- How can you change what a culture values?
- What will you do to help shape what your culture values?

Go Wireless!

Have participants form small groups of three or four members each. Ask each group to identify what its members feel that their culture values; they should also state evidence supporting their inclusion of those values (e.g., our culture values personal freedom, as evidenced by the number of personal vehicles on the road in comparison with the number of people using mass transit). Have the small groups share their identified values and supporting evidence with the large group.

Upgrade

Ask the groups to take pictures of what their members *personally* value, as well as what they feel their culture *should* value; then have them share their pictures with the entire group.

Treasure Hunting

Overview

This activity is an adaptation of geocaching, which, with the growing affordability of handheld GPS devices, has become a popular game played by people of all ages. Geocachers use handheld GPS units to locate a cache—a small, weatherproof storage container (e.g., a Tupperware container). Caches are hidden all over the world, and some are probably hidden in or close to your current town. When someone locates a cache, he or she selects an object to take from the cache, places an object of his or her choosing in the cache, and replaces the container back in its hiding place. Based on geocaching, the Treasure Hunting activity presented here encourages participants to consider what they value, and the processing questions challenge your group to consider not only the objects placed in the cache but also the personal values they hold dear.

Directions

In preparation for this activity, you will need to hide several caches. The exact number is up to you, but you should have at least two caches per team. Take your first cache (right now, it's just an empty container) and place it in a safe, hidden spot that is both near the location of the upcoming session and unlikely to be discovered by a casual passerby. We recommend hiding the cache outdoors, within 0.25 mile (0.4 kilometer) of the session location. Get the GPS coordinates for the location from your GPS device and write them down, then proceed to the next location where you would like to leave a cache. Repeat this process until you have hidden the desired number of caches. When you get to the final cache, you should leave three or four small objects (one for each member of the group), along with the coordinates for the starting location. Now, proceed backward through your caches, putting the GPS coordinates to the subsequent cache in each of the caches so that each small group participating in the activity will be able to use GPS coordinates found at a given cache to move them to the next cache and, finally, back to the starting location. This process should be repeated (but hiding caches in different locations) for each group that will be participating. There should be different "cache paths" for each group.

Before the session, ask each participant to bring an object that has some value to him or her but that he or she wouldn't mind giving away to someone else. In addition, ask participants to bring either a camera or a camera phone, as well as a handheld GPS device, cell phone with

Treasure Hunting *(continued)*

GPS capability, or portable GPS vehicle device capable of receiving input coordinates. When the participants arrive for the activity, have them form groups of three or four members each and confirm that at least one group member has a GPS device. Provide GPS coordinates to each group that will direct them to their first cache (each group should have a different first cache and subsequent cache path). Each group should use its members' GPS device(s) to locate the first cache. When a group has located its first cache, the group's members should then follow the directions they find in that cache. They should continue to follow the directions they find in each cache until they return to the original location. When a group locates the last cache in its cache path—that is, the one that contains objects—its members may each take an object from it, but they also must place the object they brought to the session into the cache.

In addition to removing items from the cache and adding items to it, each group should also create a photo essay for their journey. Simply taking pictures of the objects that they removed and added at the final cache will provide documentation of the journey and of the items that exchanged places. At the completion of the event, participants should return to the starting location and upload their digital images to a computer. Before addressing the processing questions, allow each group to share its photo essay with the rest of the large group.

Focus

Value: Every person values certain things. Some people value money, and some value service. Some people value friends, and some value solitude. Some people value tradition, and some value new ideas. Regardless of what a given person values, when we are working in teams we have to learn to understand why other people value what they do. For example, I may work on a team with a member from the Jewish community. If we are to work together effectively, it will help if I understand what is important to this member of my team. This activity helps participants look with open-minded curiosity at particular objects and the value placed on them by their owners.

Equipment

GPS unit for each group, digital camera, cache containers, objects placed in each group's final cache by facilitator, objects brought by participants to replace what they remove from their final cache

Users

Groups of 3 or 4

Processing

- How hard was this activity? What made it easy or difficult?
- What object did you bring to put in the cache? Why?
- What object did you take from the cache? Why?
- How did your group decide who would get which object from the cache?
- What were your thoughts and feelings about getting your first choice?
- What were your thoughts and feelings about not getting your first choice?
- What did the objects in the cache say about what the group does or doesn't value?
- What do you value? How would people know this?
- How can we show that we value something—or someone?

Go Wireless!

This activity can be completed as a traditional scavenger hunt, wherein the facilitator provides an initial clue and groups then work from clues that you have placed in subsequent locations. The cache is located at the last spot, and when participants find it they trade objects as in the original version of the activity.

Upgrade

Most areas in the United States are already home to caches that could easily be incorporated into this activity, and you can locate caches hidden in your area by visiting www.geocaching.com. To use this upgrade, assign each group an existing cache to locate and remind group members to take objects with which to replace anything they remove from the cache. Remind them also that they should leave the cache where they find it. When the groups return, in addition to using the processing questions provided for the original activity, you can allow each group to share about its journey. You might also consider any of several variations of geo-caching—for example, benchmark hunting, in which participants in the United States can seek out survey markers placed by the U.S. Geological Survey. You can find information about this and other variations at www. geocaching.com.

Self-Portraits

Overview

Any group is made up of individuals, and it is important for each group member to bring a certain level of self-awareness to the table. People who are unaware of their skills and abilities may not be able to help the group as much as people who are aware of their abilities can. In this activity, each group member takes pictures of images that represent herself or himself and then shares these images with one another. Through this process of identifying objects that represent the self, participants will be forced to explore who they are, which can lead to a deepened awareness of self.

Directions

Ask participants to take 5 to 10 pictures that represent themselves. The pictures can show anything, as long as the photographer feels a meaningful connection with the image. The facilitator should transfer the images to a computer so that they can be projected onto a large screen for other group members to see. Ask each person to share his or her pictures and explain the connection between the image and himself or herself.

Taking pictures that represent oneself to share can help participants become more aware of what strengths they bring to the group. A person who loves coffee shops and art may bring serenity and creativity to a group.

Focus

Self-awareness: The current generation of young people often enjoys self-expression, but rarely do they take a systematic and introspective look at the answers to questions such as, "Who am I?" and "How do others view me?" This activity provides an opportunity for participants to develop their self-awareness and explore individual issues (e.g., What are my passions? What do I spend most of my time doing? How does that affect others?) with other group members. This process of exposure and interaction gives group members a chance to increase their closeness to and understanding of each other.

Equipment
Camera or camera phone for each individual, computer, LCD projector

Users
12 to 15

Processing
- Which picture most showed you something new about someone?
- Which picture offered you the most new insight into someone?
- Which picture most had you scratching your head?
- Which picture made the most sense?
- What was it like to share yourself in this manner?
- What fears did you have about this activity?
- What did the activity teach you about yourself?
- What did the activity teach you about others?
- From the image you provided, what would you say you bring to the group?

Go Wireless!
Ask participants to collect 5 to 10 objects that represent themselves. The objects can be anything, as long as the collector feels a meaningful connection with them. Then ask participants to share their objects and explain the connection between their objects and themselves.

Upgrade
When working with a very close-knit group, you might ask group members to take pictures of objects that represent someone else in the group. The person who took the pictures can then share how they represent that person. You can suggest different categories to allow for more conversation—for example, taking pictures that represent one's work self, one's Friday night self, or one's Monday morning self.

Another upgrade involves asking participants to guess who is represented by the images on the screen before they hear the picture taker discuss the person that he or she had in mind. This variation gives all group members—not just the picture taker—the opportunity to share how they believe certain images might represent a certain person. The participant sharing the picture also learns how others perceive and how well others know him or her. For example, a group member could share an image portraying her artistic abilities, but if no other members guess she is associated with the image, the group may realize they are missing the knowledge of this persons' strength for an upcoming project. The individual may also realize she needs to speak up more about her own abilities.

The Eyes Have It

Overview

This activity promotes understanding of different perspectives by asking participants to take and then examine close-up pictures of group members' eyes; beyond that, it encourages participants to explore the metaphor

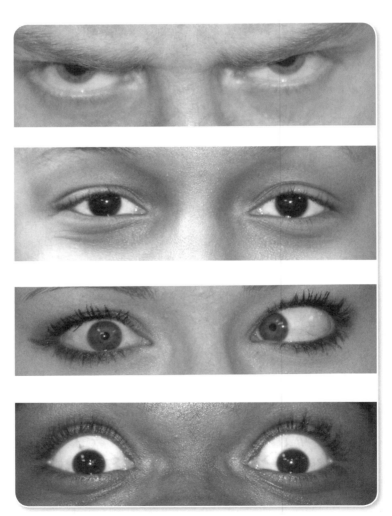

Viewing close-up images of group members' eyes promotes the discussion of different perspectives.

of seeing the world through another person's eyes. The activity upgrade helps you generate discussion that moves participants past simply seeing what others see to exploring other senses and experiences.

Directions

Before the session, take a close-up digital picture of the eyes of everyone in the group, then use photo-editing software to crop each picture so that you can see only the individual's eyes. Once you have edited all of the photographs, create a presentation with each image on a slide. During the session, show each of the images on a screen and ask the group members to identify the person; if there is disagreement, ask the participants to come to a consensus about whose eyes they are seeing.

Focus

Different perspectives: We often forget that other people see the world differently than we do, and this activity encourages participants to view situations from different perspectives. Specifically, it can be hard to "walk a mile in another person's shoes" to understand where someone else is coming from, and this activity allows a group to observe and discuss experiences from different perspectives.

Equipment

Camera (or camera phone), computer, LCD projector

Users

10 to 20

Processing

- Whose eyes were the easiest to identify? Why?
- Whose were the hardest? Why?
- What do your eyes see every day?
- What have your eyes seen?
- What have you seen that others have not?
- What have others seen that you have not?
- What can we learn from looking through another's eyes?

Go Wireless!

Ask each person to draw a picture of his or her own eyes and talk about what those eyes have seen during his or her lifetime. The processing can move into talking about the different things that each person has seen.

The Eyes Have It *(continued)*

Upgrade

Have participants take pictures of different body parts (e.g., feet, hands, head, nose, mouth) and have the group try to match the body part to the person. Ask group members to talk about what their hands have done, where their feet have walked, what ideas their head has created, what they have smelled, or what they have tasted. The electronic files of the body parts could also be combined in a presentation software such as PowerPoint or using online photo management Web sites such as Mosaic Maker (http://bighugelabs.com/mosaic.php) or Picasa (http://picasa.google.com/) to create one image that represents the entire group. For additional information on creating collages or mosaics, see Family History Collage in this chapter (p. 61).

My Collage

Overview

This activity is all about opportunities for self-reflection and self-exploration. Participants seek images that represent the answers to provided questions, then put those images together to form a collage. The activity's final step involves team building by asking the members of small groups to come together and create group collages; during this process, they are encouraged to compare their individual work with that of others in their small group.

Directions

Give participants the following list of questions and ask them to write their answers down.

- What is your first name?
- What was your first job?
- What is your favorite holiday?
- What is your favorite dessert?
- What is your favorite musical group?
- Who is your favorite celebrity?
- What is your favorite reality show?
- What is your favorite wild animal?
- What word describes you?
- What event do you most look forward to in your life?

- What is your favorite vacation spot?
- What is your favorite topic to learn about?

   Next, have participants conduct a Web search for images that fit their answers using a search engine such as Google Images or Flickr and activating the site's "safe search" feature, if it has one. For example, if a participant's first name is Colbey, he or she would search an image site for the term *Colbey.* Participants should use only those images found on the first page of results. When an appropriate image is located, it should be pasted onto one slide of a presentation software application like PowerPoint. Repeat this process for all of the images, pasting them all onto one slide in the presentation software. This can be done as creatively as individuals would like (e.g., size, location, rotation, and so on).

   Now have participants form groups of three or four members each and have each group combine its slides into one PowerPoint presentation. The presentation should consist of one slide for each group member, as well as an additional slide that combines images from the individual slides to demonstrate connections between the group's members. Finally, have each group share its presentation with the rest of the large group.

Focus

Self-reflection and self-exploration: We spend much of our time looking at other people and evaluating them and their actions; we often spend less time, however, reflecting on who *we* are and exploring and evaluating ourselves. The purpose of this activity is to encourage participants to reflect on themselves and as a result engage in self-exploration with a particular eye toward who they are and what they value. However, the activity doesn't end there. As participants work to combine their collages and identify similarities with each other, they will be drawn closer to one another.

Equipment

Computer with Internet connection (for each person), LCD projector

Users

10 to 20

Processing

Processing for this activity consists mostly of having individuals present their images to their small groups, explain why they selected the particular images they did, and explore what connections they share with others in their group as revealed in the presented images. Processing should begin with individuals sharing their personal slides and then the small group sharing their group slide. This should be repeated for all groups.

My Collage (*continued*)

Individual Questions
- What images did you select?
- Why did you select those images?
- How do those images represent you?

Group Questions
- How did you create your group slide?
- What connections did you see among members of your group?

Go Wireless!

Have participants search for images not on the Web but in magazines that you provide at the session. As participants answer questions and cut out images, each person can glue his or her images to a sheet of paper to make a traditional collage.

Upgrade

Generally follow the instructions for the original version of the activity but have participants answer questions that call for more personally revealing answers and thus promote greater self-reflection and self-exploration. Here are some possibilities:

- What is your greatest fear?
- What frustrates you the most about other people?
- What frustrates you the most about yourself?
- What is your greatest accomplishment?
- What do you wish other people knew about you?
- What was one of your childhood dreams?
- What is one of your current dreams?
- What job would you like to have for a day?
- What is your secret guilty pleasure?
- What do you value in life?
- What is your greatest hope?
- Who was your first love?

Adapted from http://kamigoroshi.net/web/meme/the-flickr-game

Bumper Sticker Philosophy

Overview

Most of us have enjoyed a good chuckle thanks to a clever bumper sticker, and this activity taps into the humor and self-expression that can often be seen in traffic. Participants learn about the importance of self-expression and how one's messages can be received by others either as intended or in a very different way.

Directions

Have participants form small groups of three or four members each and ask each group to go out and take pictures of bumper stickers or signs (e.g., posters, banners, billboards) that they find interesting; each group should define *interesting* for itself. Allow 20 to 30 minutes for the groups to do this work. When all groups have returned, allow each group to upload its images to the computer and present them to the full group, along with the group members' reasons for taking the pictures they chose.

By taking pictures of bumper stickers, participants explore self-expression and how others interpret various expressions.

Courtesy of Ross Eli Baylis

Bumper Sticker Philosophy *(continued)*

Focus
Self-expression: People choose to express themselves in a plethora of ways, and sometimes the message that one intends to send is not the message that others receive. During this activity, group members see both the messages that individuals sent (the bumper sticker or other sign) and the received message (the group members' interpretations of the sticker or sign).

Equipment
Camera or camera phone for each group, computer, LCD projector

Users
Groups of 3 or 4

Processing
- Which image was your favorite? Why?
- Is there one that you would like to have on your car right now? Why?
- Which image would most embarrass you? Why?
- Which image(s) made you angry? Why?
- What do a person's bumper stickers say about him or her?
- If you could make a bumper sticker for your car, what would it say? Why?

Go Wireless!
Have participants form small groups of three or four members each and ask each group to write down the messages from several bumper stickers that they find interesting (each group should define *interesting* for itself). When all of the groups have returned, allow each group to share the messages it recorded, along with rationales for the selections.

Upgrade
Have participants form small groups of three or four members each and ask each group to search various social networking Web sites for bumper stickers or flair that they find interesting (each group should define *interesting* for itself). When all of the groups have finished, allow each group to present its findings, along with rationales for the selections.

A Picture Is Worth a Thousand Words

Overview

This activity encourages conversations related to diversity and stereotypes as group members attempt to develop captions for pictures that the facilitator presents. The processing questions for this activity challenge participants to explore stereotypes that may have colored their thinking as they developed their captions; they also encourage participants to value diversity by appreciating different interpretations of the pictures.

Directions

In preparation for this activity, select several (up to 10) images that present some form of action. You can find suitable images by using Google Images or Flickr to search online for funny pictures, pictures that include animals, or pictures that involve some form of action (involving sports or other activities). One word of caution: When searching, make sure to use a filter or safe search feature.

Crafting a caption for a given picture can help groups discuss stereotypes placed on people.

A Picture Is Worth a Thousand Words *(continued)*

To begin the activity itself, have participants form small groups of three or four members each; then, one image at a time, present all of the images you have selected. The easiest way to do this is to use presentation software such as PowerPoint. As each picture appears on the screen, ask each group to write a caption that describes what is happening in the image. The captions can be funny or serious, but in either case they should be inoffensive and representative of the group members' feelings about the image. After all of the images have been presented, show them all again, this time allowing each group to share its caption with the larger group.

Focus

Diversity and stereotypes: Even when viewing the same image, people often respond very differently. This activity encourages participants to express their own thoughts and to embrace others' thoughts, which might be different from their own. In addition, as the groups share their captions, opportunities arise for participants to discuss stereotypes demonstrated in the images or reinforced through the captions.

Equipment

Preselected pictures, computer, LCD projector

Users

Groups of 3 or 4

Processing

Processing for this activity begins with having the small groups share their captions.

- Were any of the captions exactly the same? Why or why not?
- Were any of the captions similar? Why or why not?
- For which image did the captions differ most from each other? Why might this have been the case?
- Why were so few captions exactly the same?
- What went into the development of your group's captions?
- How did your personal identity and personal history influence your captioning of the photos?
- Were any of the captions 100 percent accurate? Is it possible to know?
- When have you put a "caption" on someone in real life? Was it accurate? How do you know?
- What can we learn from this activity about putting captions on other people?

Go Wireless!

Instead of searching the Web for pictures, select four to six images from printed magazines to provide to each group (i.e., each group should have its own set of the same four to six images). Once the groups have their images, proceed with the directions as listed above.

Upgrade

Have participants form small groups of three or four members each and ask them to go out and take their own action-oriented pictures, funny pictures, or emotional pictures. Each group should take about five or six pictures. Once all groups have returned to the meeting location, have each group create a caption for each image that its members would like to present. When all groups have captioned their images, have each group share its images and captions with the larger group.

Caption Action

Overview

This activity gives participants the chance to explore different perspectives as they attempt to create images to fit a provided caption that is intentionally ambiguous; thus this activity is the inverse of A Picture Is Worth a Thousand Words. The ultimate goal here is to help group members see how people can interpret the same prompt (in this case, a caption) very differently—a useful exercise to help groups learn to celebrate differences among one another in the group.

Directions

In preparation for this activity, create 8 to 10 captions for hypothetical pictures. For example: "Man eating plant," "The incredible shrinking team," "A dime a dozen," "Surf's up, dude!" To begin the activity, have participants form groups of three or four members each and provide each group with the list of captions. The task for each group is to take a picture to fit each caption. Images should not be offensive and should creatively fit the substance of the provided caption. When all groups have created their images, have them upload their images to a computer from which they can be shown to the full group via an LCD projector. Each group should present its image for each caption.

Caption Action *(continued)*

Creating a photo for a given caption such as "the incredible shrinking team" helps participants see how individuals or groups of people can interpret the same idea differently.

Courtesy of Ross Eli Baylis

Focus
Different perspectives: Even when reading the same words, people can interpret them very differently. This activity encourages participants to express their creativity and interpret language in a way that makes sense to them. Even if some images are the same or very similar, each group's perspective (e.g., interpretation of the caption or the image selected) will be different. These different perspectives should be discussed and embraced.

Equipment
Camera or camera phone for each group, computer, LCD projector

Users
Groups of 3 or 4

Processing
Processing for this activity begins with having each group share its pictures; along the way, the other groups guess which caption a given picture represents.
- Which picture fit its caption best?
- Which picture was the most original?
- Which picture did you need to have explained to you in order for you to understand the caption? Why?

- Did any of the groups create the same pictures? If so, what was it about the relevant image(s) that made this happen?
- What went into the development of your group's pictures?
- How did your identity and your personal history influence your creation of pictures for the captions?
- How do different perspectives create growth within groups?
- How do different perspectives create difficulties within groups? How can these difficulties be resolved productively?

Go Wireless!

Using your list of created captions, ask the small groups to create a still image using only the members of the group. This can be done in a variety of ways: groups can pose themselves, draw the scene, and so on. When all groups have completed the activity, have them present their images for each caption. During these presentations, each group should guess which caption matches a given still image.

Upgrade

Have participants form groups of three or four members each, then have each group create five or six captions that could describe a hypothetical image (start by providing an example or two). Next, the members of each group should create a picture to fit each caption, either by taking a picture or by creating their own image using any medium *except* any form of drawing (which they would then take a picture of). For instance, a group might find several objects and create a sculpture that represents the caption; members of another group might use their bodies to create an image. The images should be inoffensive and should fit the substance of the associated caption. When all groups have completed the activity, have them upload their images to a computer from which they can be projected via an LCD projector. Each group should present its image for each caption.

Family History Collage

Overview

While generally similar to My Collage, this activity differs fundamentally in that it shifts the focus from the participant to the participant's family. It is important to remember that people come from somewhere and that we have backgrounds and experiences that developed from our family situation. Family History Collage embraces this aspect of our identities

Family History Collage *(continued)*

and challenges participants both to explore who they are specifically in relation to their family (however that term may be defined in the group you are working with) and to connect themselves to the group with which they are currently working.

Directions

Prior to the session, ask participants to bring electronic images that represent their family (they can bring images on a phone, digital camera, CD, or USB flash drive).

Have participants form groups of three or four members each, then ask participants to combine their images with the images of others in their small group. Create a Flickr account to upload each image into the Mosaic Maker at Big Huge Labs (http://bighugelabs.com/mosaic.php). You will need to change the number of columns and rows to accommodate the necessary number of pictures. Once all of your images have been found and inserted into the Mosaic Maker, click Create. Each group should then save or upload their picture to Flickr. Once all of the images have been saved or uploaded, allow each small group to share their created mosaic with the whole group.

Focus

Interconnectedness and community: Even though it is becoming easier and easier to remain connected to people via technology, we still sometimes fail to see and make use of our existing connections. Sometimes we share commonalities with people that we are unaware of, and in some cases we may even be part of a community without realizing it (e.g., college students who are away from home become a part of the community where their school is located, but they might not recognize this). This activity is designed to help group members see how they are connected to one another and how they are all part of a larger community.

Equipment

Several computers with Internet connections, LCD projector

Users

Groups of 3 or 4

Processing

- What similarities did you see between members of your small group?
- What differences did you see within your small group?
- What similarities and differences did you see between members of all the groups?

- Why is it important to understand the idea of connectedness with those around us?
- How can technology help us become or remain connected with one another?
- How can technology hinder our connectedness?
- How can being connected with others help us?
- How can you connect with those around you?

Go Wireless!

Prior to the activity, ask group members to bring pictures of themselves and their families (specifically, copies that they don't mind having cut or otherwise damaged). To help participants who forget to bring pictures or who feel that they didn't bring enough images, you can provide magazines from which participants can cut out images that represent their family. All of the collected images (from home and from the magazines) can be taped or glued to a large piece of paper to represent the interconnected nature of the group.

Upgrade

Once all of the groups have developed their interconnected image, have them combine all of their images into one large image for the group as a whole. This process takes considerable time and work, because participants will have to work together to create it on one computer, which means that there may not be room for all group members to participate physically in designing the image (there's only one keyboard). Thus we recommend allowing the group to select one person to serve as the artist and perform the specific computer manipulations of the images. We also recommend that you project the images onto a large screen so that all members can observe what the artist is doing and participate actively, via discussion, in the creation of the final image.

Emotional Expressions

Overview

The title of this activity directly expresses its purpose. In asking participants to take pictures of people who are acting out specific emotions, the activity sets the stage for participants to conduct a conversation about the nature of emotions and the importance of understanding other group members' emotions.

Emotional Expressions *(continued)*

Directions

Have participants form small groups of three or four members each and give each group a digital camera and a list of emotions (e.g., happy, sad, afraid, excited, bored, confused, angry, nervous, and so on; the facilitator can search online for "emotional expressions" for more examples). Ask the groups to go out and ask strangers to pose for a picture while displaying an emotion from the list. Encourage groups to find different people for different emotions. After each group has returned with pictures of people demonstrating 8 to 10 emotions, upload the images to a computer. Then give each group a chance to present its pictures while the other groups guess which emotion is being expressed by the pictured person.

Taking pictures of different emotional expressions helps groups discuss the importance of discerning nonverbal cues and understanding the role our emotions play in teamwork.

Focus

Identifying emotions: Emotions can be difficult to talk about and thus can be ignored or misinterpreted for a considerable period of time. When members of a group fail to discuss important emotions, the group can fall prey to friction and poor performance. By asking group members to identify different emotions, you help them become more comfortable with talking about their own and each other's emotions, thus improving the group's cohesion. Groups that are more cohesive are more likely to perform at higher levels.

Equipment

Camera or camera phone for each group, computer, LCD projector

Users

Groups of 3 or 4

Processing

- Which emotions were easiest to identify? Why?
- Which emotions were hardest to identify? Why?
- Were you personally able to discern others' emotional responses very well?
- When have you misinterpreted an individual's emotional response? Why did this happen? What was the result?
- Are some people's emotions more difficult to read than others'? If so, why do you think this is?
- What fears did you have about approaching strangers and asking them to demonstrate emotions?
- What did this activity teach you about yourself?
- What did this activity teach you about others?
- What did this activity teach you about identifying emotions?

Go Wireless!

Have participants form small groups of three or four members each and give each group a list of emotions. Ask each group to select 8 to 10 emotions that its members would like to demonstrate to the larger group (as in charades—that is, without speaking). Give each group time to demonstrate its chosen emotions to the larger group; along the way, the other groups should guess which emotion is being expressed.

Upgrade

Have participants form small groups of three or four members each and give each group a digital camera and a list of eight emotions. Ask the groups to take pictures of themselves displaying each emotion on the list, then upload the resulting images to a computer. Next, have each group present its pictures while the other groups guess which emotion is being expressed in each image.

Freeze-Frame

Overview

This seemingly simple activity provides a challenging experience in paying attention to detail. It requires certain group members to observe others and try to remember how they are posed. Processing questions for this activity focus on attending to detail and subtleties and challenge participants

Freeze-Frame *(continued)*

to make comparisons between this activity and personal experiences in which they have overlooked details and faced problems as a result.

Directions

Have participants form two groups, then have the two groups stand facing away from each other. Quietly tell the members of one team (team A) that you are going to ask them to creatively pose as a group; in addition to posing, they should make subtle changes in their appearance (e.g., trading shoes, watches, jewelry, hats). Next, allow team A to huddle in order to discuss a plan of action while you provide members of team B with their instructions. Quietly tell team B that team A is going to creatively pose as a group. Team B will have 1 minute to observe team A's pose in order to remember as many details as possible (including body position, body arrangement, and clothing). Once the directions have been provided to both teams, have team A strike its pose. While team A is arranging itself, team B should face *away* from team A; team B can use this time to discuss strategy. Before team B has an opportunity to view the pose, take a picture of team A's pose. Then allow team B to have its 1 minute for observing team A's pose. Members of team B may not touch anyone on team A, but they may approach and walk around team A.

Re-creating the pose of a group of people helps participants think about real-life situations in which attention to details are important.

When the allotted minute has passed, team B should turn away from team A, and the members of team A should arrange themselves into another position and switch back to their original items of clothing. Team B now has 5 minutes to rearrange the members of team A in order to reconstruct team A's creative pose. Members of team B are allowed to touch members of team A during this reconstruction phase, but they should ask before doing so. Members of team B may also ask members of team A to rearrange themselves in a certain way or change certain articles of clothing in an attempt to have them match the original pose. When team B's members believe that they have team A in the correct position, take a picture of this pose.

Now, load the picture of team A's original pose and the picture of team B's reconstruction of that pose onto a computer and show them side by side. Allow the members of team B to see if they can identify mistakes or inaccuracies in their reconstruction, then allow team A to help with any details that team B missed. If time allows, do the activity again with the teams reversing their roles.

Focus

Attention to detail: Given the ease and speed with which members of the current generation of young people can access information, they sometimes find it challenging to attend to smaller but important details. This activity requires participants to calm down, develop a plan, and concentrate on smaller details that might easily be overlooked—all in the face of a deadline (the 1-minute observation period). In a world where people are bombarded by information, it is a valuable skill to be able to slow oneself down even in the midst of deadlines and chaos.

Equipment

Camera, computer, LCD projector

Users

10 to 20

Processing

- What were the obvious changes?
- Why were they so easy to notice?
- What were the subtle changes?
- What made them so hard to notice?
- For team A: What changes did team B's members observe that you did not expect them to?
- What was your strategy for catching subtle changes?

Freeze-Frame *(continued)*

- Were you so focused on noticing subtle changes that you missed obvious ones? Why did this happen?
- What are some situations in life where you might fail to observe the details?
- What are some situations in life where you might fail to observe the obvious?
- How do we sometimes see but fail to notice?
- How can we better attend to both the details and the obvious in daily life?

Go Wireless!
Only one change is needed: When it comes time to correct the reconstructed image, simply ask team A to explain the inaccuracies. This modification works well in the absence of a camera and LCD screen.

Upgrade
To increase the activity's difficulty and help your group focus on issues of communication as well as attending to detail, follow all of the original instructions but divide team B into one subgroup that is blindfolded and one that is not. The group that is not blindfolded observes team A's pose, then, once the allotted minute for observation has passed, team A rearranges itself as described in the instructions for the original version of the activity. Next, members of the blindfolded group remove their blindfolds and, based only on oral instructions from the nonblindfolded members of their team, attempt to reconstruct the original pose from team A.

Based on George Siler, 1994, *Centrifuge games with a purpose*, page 82.

Where in the World Am I?

Overview
Gaining perspective can be a challenge for individuals in groups because we don't always understand where people are coming from, and this activity allows participants to see the importance of understanding perspective. As participants examine images that depict common locations from various angles and distances, they quickly see how difficult it can be to identify even a familiar sight without the correct perspective. This metaphor

is carried through in the activity's processing phase, wherein participants are encouraged to consider instances where they have had difficulty with perspective and to explore strategies for maintaining perspective.

Directions

Prior to the session, choose 10 locations, then for each location take or find five photographs or illustrations of the location that do not immediately give it away—for example, a local coffee shop, a local sports arena, the Grand Canyon, Mount Rushmore, or the White House. We recommend taking pictures of local businesses and landmarks, since they are likely to hold the most meaning for your group and be the easiest to get suitable pictures of.

Have participants form groups of three or four members each. Explain to the groups that you are going to show five images of each location and that they will have 15 seconds to view each image. The images will be presented one at a time, and, as the images for a given location accumulate, it will of course become easier to identify that location. When the members of any small group identify the location, they should write down their answer and hand it to the facilitator. For correctly identifying the location after seeing the first image, a group receives 50 points; after seeing the second image, 40 points; after seeing the third image, 30 points; after seeing the fourth image, 20 points; and after seeing the final image, 10 points. If a group guesses incorrectly, it loses 20 points.

After the rules have been explained, proceed to the first image of the first location and continue until you have gone through all of the chosen locations. We recommend that you present the images via presentation software such as PowerPoint or Keynote.

Focus

Perspective: We all lose perspective sometimes. We get used to seeing objects in a certain way, from a certain angle, and when that angle changes—or when our situation changes—we may have difficulty with seeing and comprehending. This activity encourages participants to see objects in different ways, to see something new in something old, and thus to see life in a different way.

Equipment

Computer with Internet connection, LCD projector

Users

Groups of 3 or 4

Where in the World Am I?   *(continued)*

Processing

- Which group won? Which group lost?
- Was winning or losing important to you? Why or why not?
- What made groups successful in their identifications?
- What made it difficult to identify the images?
- What made it easy to identify the images?
- Did it bother you when you couldn't identify an image but someone else did right away? Why or why not? If so, how did you handle it?
- Is it important to try looking at life experiences from various viewpoints? Why or why not? If so, what can be gained from doing so?
- What can be lost in looking at our life experiences from the same viewpoint every time?

Go Wireless!

Prior to the session, print or cut out parts of large pictures of a location that can be shown to the group. The rest of the directions remain the same.

Upgrade

Rather than using five images of a location, repeat the activity with images of people, animals, cars, or any other subject that lends itself to viewing from multiple perspectives.

3

Internet Activities

The Internet has revolutionized the ways in which many people communicate—what, when, and with whom. People share their life events through pictures; posts on blogs, Facebook, MySpace, Twitter, and so on; and updates sent to friends they haven't seen in person in 20 years and even complete strangers around the globe. While driving the information highway, one can learn how to fix a leaky faucet or find the inspiration behind a popular song. Given these vast possibilities, the Internet also serves as the setting for countless instances in which users face communication challenges such as miscommunication, misinterpretation, and misinformation. The activities presented in this chapter encourage users to see the Internet as a tool that they can use for growing in relationship with fellow team members and others by thinking about how pictures, posts, and other information can be interpreted in various ways.

For many activities presented here, the facilitator must have use of a computer with an Internet connection, as well as an LCD projector to display the computer screen's contents for the group to see. Some activities that involve multiple groups require access to more than one computer, and some require that group members or the facilitator display material via presentation software such as PowerPoint.

This chapter contains the following activities:

Behind the Seen

Overview

At a glance, improving one's awareness of current and historical events may not seem directly connected to team building, but this activity uses such events as a platform for discussion of your group's history and culture. By using the Internet to explore and gain awareness of various events—to look behind what is seen—participants will be encouraged to explore their own contexts in a similar fashion. Groups whose members are aware of their history and culture are more likely to forge a shared vision for the group's direction because they have an understanding of what is of value and importance to their group members.

Directions

Have participants form small groups of three or four members each. Ask each group to quietly (not letting other teams know what they are doing) search the Internet for an image of a national monument, the name of a leader in the Civil Rights Movement, a popular song, a female author, a current religious leader, or a current politician (that is, assign one category to each group). Each group should e-mail its image to you, and you should

Using the Internet to explore answers to questions regarding given events and people helps groups understand the importance of having an awareness of their own history and culture.

then forward that image to another group so that each group has an image from another group. Once each group has its new image, ask the group members to use the Internet to answer the following questions about it:

National Monument

- What is the name of the national monument?
- Where is it located?
- Who created it?
- Why was it erected?
- What can we learn from the rationale behind the construction of this monument?
- Was there any controversy surrounding its establishment?
- Why select it for this list?

Civil Rights Leader

- Who is the person?
- What did the person do to advance civil rights?
- How was the person received by the general public at that time?

Behind the Seen *(continued)*

- Where was the person from?
- What was the person's education?
- What made the person a leader?
- Did a particular event propel this individual into leadership? If so, what was it? If not, how did the person rise to prominence?
- Why select the person for this list?
- What can we learn about leadership from this individual?

Popular Song

- What is the name of the song?
- Who wrote it?
- When was it first released?
- What was the inspiration behind it?
- What can we learn from the meaning of and inspiration behind this song?
- How many artists have recorded the song?
- Why is it popular?
- Why select this song for this list?

Female Author

- Who is she?
- What type of writing does she do?
- What is her most popular work?
- Where is she from?
- When was she first published?
- What made her work popular?
- Why select her for this list?
- What can we learn about gender from this individual?

Religious Leader

- Who is the person?
- What has the person done for religion?
- How has the person been received in the media?
- Where is the person from?
- What is the person best known for?
- Why select him or her for this list?
- What can we learn about religion and acceptance from this individual?

Politician

- Who is the person?
- What state or area does this person represent?
- When was the person first elected?
- How long has the person been in office?
- What legislation has the person influenced?
- What is the person most known for?
- How has the person's work benefited others?
- Why select him or her for this list?
- What can we learn from this individual about service to others?

Focus

Historical and current events awareness: This activity deepens participants' understanding of historical and contemporary characters and issues. By examining issues and people of cultural relevance, participants can feel more connected to their culture and develop greater understanding of their placement within the culture.

Equipment

Computer with Internet connection for each group

Users

Groups of 3 or 4

Processing

Processing for this activity begins with the questions that each group answers for its particular topic. Once a group has generated its answers, its members can present their questions and answers to the other groups, who are free to offer their own responses to the questions (e.g., someone from another group might share why he or she thinks a certain national monument was selected for the activity). After all the groups have shared, pose the following questions to everyone:

- What is the culture and history of this (overall) group?
- What can we learn by being aware of our history and culture?

Go Wireless!

Rather than giving each small group a different topic, you could also select one topic for all of the small groups to address, then provide participants with magazines, newspapers, and other printed resources to use in researching it. Have the small groups answer the same questions

Behind the Seen *(continued)*

provided for the original version of the activity and share their responses with the rest of the larger group.

Upgrade

For an increased challenge, have the groups explore controversial or otherwise intense figures, monuments, or songs (e.g., Fidel Castro, Moammar Gadhafi, Hugo Chávez, the United States Holocaust Memorial Museum, "I Kissed a Girl" by Katy Perry).

What Do You See Here?

Overview

This activity promotes understanding of different perspectives by asking participants to explore images found on social networking Web sites. When participants gain understanding of fellow group members' different perceptions and interpretive approaches, they also gain greater understanding of rationales behind decisions made within the group. This activity also encourages each participant to examine how others may perceive images found on his or her own social networking page.

Directions

Have participants form groups of three or four members each and ask them to search various social networking sites to find pictures of people engaged in the following activities:

- Doing something athletic
- Doing something brave
- Doing something funny
- Dancing
- Attending a sporting event
- Wearing glasses
- Being silly
- Spending time with family
- Wearing a funny hat
- Lying on the beach
- Playing a video game
- Visiting a foreign country
- Celebrating a birthday
- Having a nonalcoholic drink

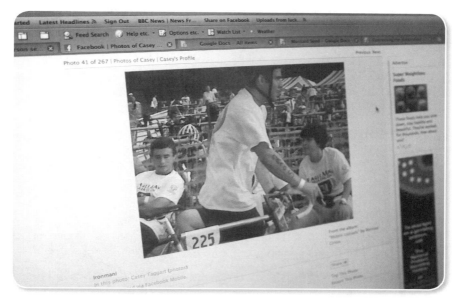

Searching social networking sites for photo ideas gives participants an opportunity to discuss perceptions and grow in understanding of each other.

- Playing music
- Watching a movie
- Eating fruit
- Canoeing
- Tubing
- Skiing
- Riding in a fancy car
- Petting an animal
- Visiting a museum

As each group locates appropriate images, its members should use software such as PowerPoint to insert each one into a presentation. Once each group has prepared its presentation, have the groups share their findings with the larger group.

Focus

Perceptions: All of the activities in the image list can be interpreted in different ways, and the interpretations chosen by a given group will depend on its members' particular perceptions. For example, "petting an animal" could involve petting either a live or stuffed (toy) animal, and "wearing a funny hat" could be interpreted as involving a hat with lots of feathers sticking out of it or one with an animal tail protruding from it. By working to understand others' perceptions of such stimuli, we can better understand the variety that characterizes the ways in which other people see the world. When we understand perceptions, we can better understand why group members may make some of their decisions, and such understanding allows groups to grow and to function more effectively and more efficiently.

Equipment
Computer with Internet connection for each group, LCD projector

Users
Groups of 3 or 4

Processing
To begin processing this activity, have each group present its selected images. For further processing, you can use the following questions:

- Why did you select the particular photos you did for your presentation?
- What do these photos say about the people in them?
- If this picture was my only source of knowledge about a person, what might I think of him or her?
- If you know this person, does the image portrayed in the picture match what you know about him or her?
- What other mediums do we use to express ourselves to others (besides social networking sites)?
- What is the image that you are portraying about yourself to this group?
- Is that the image you want to portray?
- How can you portray the image you would like to other people?

Go Wireless!
Generally follow the directions for the original version but have the small groups cut out magazine pictures of people doing the indicated activities. The small groups can paste their chosen images onto a piece of poster board in order to share them with the larger group.

Upgrade
Generally follow the directions for the original version but have the small groups find pictures only of *people in the group* (either the small group or the larger group) doing the indicated activities. This approach gives participants a glimpse into some of the activities in which their fellow group members have engaged, and this sharing of experiences helps group members create a closer bond among themselves.

E-terpretations

Overview

At one time or another, everyone in your group has probably received an e-mail that was hard to interpret. Indeed, the very nature of e-mail often makes it difficult to determine the sender's intended meaning. This activity presents participants with sample e-mails that could have many different meanings and challenges them to identify some of those meanings. Since many groups use e-mail as a means of communication between members, this chance to explore how easily e-mails can be misinterpreted may help your group improve the effectiveness of its communication.

Directions

Have participants form groups of three or four members each. Provide each group with two or three e-mails (preferably different from other groups) with rich potential for varied interpretation (see figure 3.1). As the groups read and review each e-mail, they should answer the following questions:

- What is the message's overt message?
- Is there a covert message? If so, what is it, and how do you know?
- What is the message's tone?
- How would you feel if you received this message?

Focus

Interpreting meaning: Any message can be interpreted in various ways—especially e-mail messages (as well as other forms of electronic communication) because we do not have body language or voice tone to help us interpret meaning. One dimension of interpretation involves how favorably we interpret what we read—favorably to ourselves, perhaps, or unfavorably to the author. For example, if I receive an e-mail from a student that includes the sentence, "I need to meet with you today to discuss the grade you gave me," I can interpret the statement in different ways. If I am having a good day and have plenty of time in my schedule, I may interpret it as indicating that the student is frustrated and is looking to me for assistance (a very positive interpretation). However, if I am having a bad day and feeling pressed for time, I may look at that same e-mail, home in on the phrase "grade you gave me," and assume that the student is unwilling to accept responsibility for the grade earned (a very negative response). In this activity, participants are asked to interpret a series of e-mails designed to be humorous yet thought-provoking.

Equipment

Computer, LCD projector

Users

Groups of 3 or 4

Processing

Processing for this activity begins with each group reporting its responses to the questions about each message it reviewed.

- What e-mail messages have you received that required you to actively interpret the tone?
- What are the difficulties with interpreting the tone of an e-mail message?
- Have you ever interpreted a message incorrectly?
- Is it possible to intentionally convey a certain tone in an e-mail message? If so, how?
- How have you tried purposefully to convey tone in an e-mail message? If so, how did it go?
- What messages are best sent through e-mail?
- What messages are best sent by other means?

Go Wireless!

Rather than using an LCD projector to present the e-mail messages, pass out printed messages.

Upgrade

Have participants bring in examples of e-mail messages that they have received or sent where some question of interpretation is involved. To respect the privacy of the parties involved, all names should be removed or marked out.

E-mail Interpretation

Sample 1

Dear Sir/Madam:

Permit me to inform you of our desire in going into business relationship with you.

We got your contact from an internet search with the aid of information from British chamber of commerce and industry. I prayed over it and selected your name among other names due to it's esteeming nature and the recommendations given to us as a reputable and trustworthy person we can do business with and by their recommendations I must not hesitate to confide in you for this simple and sincere business. Although our intentions was not revealed. I am Johnson Cole. Mutumba Membe, the only child of late Mr. Peter Mutumba Membe, my father was a very wealthy black farmer based in Zimbabwe before he was brutally murdered in a land dispute in his country as result of land act reform by Zimbabwean president Robert Mugabe.

The new land act reform which affected the white and black farmers, resulting to massive killings by war veterans and lunatics in the society and as a result my father was killed. But as my father foresaw the looming danger on the 21st October 1999 in Zimbabwe, he told me and my mother that he has deposited us $29,000,000 (twenty nine million united states dollars) in one private security company in Europe, that the money was meant for the purchase of new machineries for mechanized agriculture for the Zimbabwean farmers movement and new farms in Swaziland. My mother and i has since the death of my father on 29th June 2000 Seeking political asylum in Europe in a camp here in London. As an illiterate my mother called me on her side and told me that my father has made me his next of kin in the certificate of deposit as his only son. He also explained to me that it was because of this wealth that I might be killed by his associates, that i should seek for a foreign partner in a country of my choice where I will transfer this money and use it for investment purpose, (such as real estate management) I am honorably seeking your assistance in the following ways.

Figure 3.1 Sample e-mails for interpretation.

From B.D. Wolfe and C. Penton Sparkman, 2010, *Team-building activities for the digital age: Using technology to develop effective groups* (Champaign, IL: Human Kinetics).

1. To provide a bank account where this money would be transferred to

2. To serve as the guardian of this fund since I am a boy of 24 years

3. To make arrangement for me to come over to your country after the Money has been transferred.

As an asylum seeker we are not permitted to have bank accounts through-out the territorial zones of United Kingdom. Moreover, I am willing to offer you some % of the total sum as compensation for your effort/input after the successful transfer of this fund to your nominated account overseas. Furthermore, you can indicate your option towards assisting me as I believe that this transaction would be concluded within seven (7) days, please signify interest to assist me. I shall be willing to communicate with you on phone in due course.

Thanks for your mutual understanding.

Regards,

JOHNSON COLE

Sample 2

I have been reading your reports, particularly in South East Asia and I have to say they are incredibly poor. You are from an English speaking country (the U.S.A) presumably you are in your early twenties, so why is your English at the level of a mentally challenged five year old child. I cannot understand any of your ideas. If you want to set up a website with informative material please make sure you can actually write. Your con-clusions and ideas on Michael Moore and Europe are the sort of drivel I would expect from Cletus the Slack Jawed Hick, with no meaning except an obvious lack of cognitive ability. Your lack of understanding concerning the English language is an example of the failed public schooling system in America. I suggest you take elementary English lessons before embarking on another garbled blogging nightmare.

Figure 3.1 *(continued)*

From B.D. Wolfe and C. Penton Sparkman, 2010, *Team-building activities for the digital age: Using technology to develop effective groups* (Champaign, IL: Human Kinetics).

Quotable Quotes

Overview

Emphasis on personalization and self-expression has exploded with the growth of the World Wide Web. This activity asks participants to select and rank-order quotations found on social networking pages in order to explore how they express themselves. It also gives them practice in consensus building as they work to agree on which quotations to select as a group.

Directions

Have the participants form teams of three or four members each, then direct each team to scour social networking sites for the best quotes (i.e., those deemed best by the team). Each team determines its own search methods, with one caveat: They may *not* use any of the quotes on their own pages. After all teams have made their selections, have each team share its top five with the rest of the larger group.

Focus

Self-expression and consensus: People choose to express themselves through different means, and with the proliferation of social networking sites more and more people are expressing their personal, religious, and political views in new and alternative ways. This activity asks participants to explore how quotations from social networking pages express people's individuality. Group members also have opportunities for developing consensus as they navigate the potentially choppy waters of their selection process. The term *best* is intentionally left undefined, and group members will likely find that they sometimes disagree about which quotations are in fact best and thus that they must practice the art of compromise in order to determine the group's top five.

Equipment

Computer with Internet access for each team

Users

Groups of 3 or 4

Processing

Self-Expression

- Which quotation did you personally like the best?
- Which quotation do you wish you had on your page?
- What does a person's quotation say about him or her?

- Would you be embarrassed if someone you know—for example, your mom, dad, brother, sister, grandmother, or grandfather—read your quotations?
- What do your quotations say about you?

Consensus

- How did the group determine what *best* meant?
- What process did the group use to rank-order the quotes?
- Was everyone heard during your group's selection process? Was everyone's opinion valued?
- Is consensus building important? Why or why not?
- When might it be important to build consensus?
- How can you develop consensus in situations outside of this activity?

Go Wireless!

Ask participants to arrive with quotations in hand; alternatively, provide participants with magazines (e.g., *Reader's Digest*) that include lists of quotations from which they can choose. Participants should still form teams of three or four members each and come to consensus regarding the best quotations, then share their selections with the rest of the overall group.

Upgrade

Direct each team to use quotations only from its members' own social networking pages. This level of self-exposure can enable participants to gain insight into how other group members think. Viewing each other's quotations and addressing the processing questions together helps group members gain greater understanding of one another and draw closer together as a group.

Survey Says

Overview

No two people see the world in the same way, and this activity reinforces that lesson by means of an approach made popular in a famous game show. By polling your group members (and, if you use the activity upgrade, polling others), you will help your group learn about seeing different perspectives and explore the importance of understanding and respecting those different perspectives.

Directions

Prior to the session, prepare questions for your group. You should use at least 10 questions for the activity, but you should prepare more than 10 questions for the survey. Preparing additional questions provides some flexibility in case there are difficulties with responses on some of the polls. Here are a few sample questions:

- What is your favorite musical group?
- What is your favorite TV show?
- What is your favorite movie?
- What is your favorite book?
- What is your favorite song?
- What is your favorite dessert?
- What is your favorite late-night snack?
- Where is your favorite place to vacation?
- How many hours of sleep do you get each day?
- What is your favorite sport to play?
- What is your favorite sport to watch?
- What type of car do you drive?

Taking a poll can be a fun way to highlight similarities and differences in the likes or values of people.

Once you have completed your question list, visit Poll Everywhere at www.polleverywhere.com. This Web site allows you to create simple polls that participants can answer via text message. Use the site to create several polls (a separate poll will be needed for each question) asking participants to identify their top choices in various categories. As participants respond, the site will collect information regarding their choices.

After collecting all of the information, rank-order the responses in each category according to their popularity. For example, for the question "Who is your favorite music group?" responses may range from U2 to the Beatles to the Jonas Brothers to Akon. If three people selected U2 as their favorite group, one selected the Beatles, seven selected the Jonas Brothers, and eight selected Akon, you would order them as follows: 8 Akon, 7 Jonas

Survey Says *(continued)*

Brothers, 3 U2, 1 Beatles. If you like, you can convert these numbers to percentages: 42 percent Akon; 37 percent Jonas Brothers; 16 percent U2; 5 percent Beatles. Graphically present the information collected from the polls in a PowerPoint presentation. Once you have collected all of this information, you can play Survey Says; if possible, you might choose to do the survey work several weeks in advance so that the participants are less likely to remember their exact responses.

At the time of the activity, divide the group into two teams. Call one member from each team forward and ask them to guess the top-ranked response in a given category according to the group's survey results. For example, if the survey asked each respondent to name his or her favorite sport to play, you would ask the two team representatives to guess the *group's* favorite sport to play. Rather than using a buzzer, have the selected member from each team text the response to the facilitator's phone. The team with the higher-ranked answer (or in the case of the same answer, the team whose text was received first) is allowed to have each member supply another answer for the question. Team members supply answers individually with no help from their teammates, and these follow-up answers are given to the facilitator orally (no texting needed). If a team member supplies an answer that is not included in the group's rank-ordered survey responses, the team gets a strike. If a team gets three strikes, the opposing team then gets an opportunity to give one more correct answer (i.e., an answer that showed up somewhere in the group's rank-ordered list) to win the round. One person states this answer for the opposing team, but all team members are allowed to collaborate in deciding the answer. If this team gives an answer that is included in the group's survey responses, it wins the round; if the answer is not included, then the other team wins the round. The game continues in this manner until at least 10 of the questions have been used.

Focus

Different perspectives: What one person likes or values is not necessarily what another person likes or values. This activity uses a fun, well-known game to highlight both similarities and differences between individuals.

Equipment

One cell phone per team, one cell phone for the facilitator, computer with Internet connection, LCD projector

Users

Two groups of 10 to 12

Processing

- Which poll result surprised you the most?
- Which poll result didn't surprise you at all?
- How do your preferences compare generally with those of the group?
- Why do we compare our preferences with those of other people? Is this a good thing? Why or why not?
- What can we learn by comparing our preferences with those of other people?

Go Wireless!

To adapt this activity for a low-tech environment, you can use printed surveys to collect information from your group. Then, when playing the game, participants can use a buzzer or bell to signify who responded first and thus gets to offer an answer.

Upgrade

One creative way to upgrade this activity is to survey a larger sample of people (you would do so in advance). You might do this by means of Google Docs, which requires that you create a Gmail account. Once you have created your account, visit http://docs.google.com and click the "New" button on the left-hand side of the screen. Then select "Form" from the drop-down menu and follow the on-screen prompts to create your online survey. When you have finished creating your survey instrument, click on the "Email this Form" button in the upper right-hand corner in order to send the survey to groups of people that you have working relationships with.

Mirror, Mirror, on the Wall

Overview

This activity asks participants to take an introspective look at their social networking pages in an effort to view them through the eyes of a stranger. Participants are asked to do so by answering several critical questions: What is this person known for? What does this person value? Is this person committed to the growth of other people? Thus the activity gives you a fresh way to help participants explore the fact that being committed to each other's growth is vital to the group's ongoing success. The upgrade for this activity challenges group members to see how the friends they list on their social networking pages help define who they are.

Mirror, Mirror, on the Wall *(continued)*

Directions

This activity works best when participants complete it prior to the session and then use the group meeting to discuss their experiences with the activity.

Ask participants to review their social networking page (any who do not have their own page can review someone else's) from the perspective of a third person who knows nothing about them. Participants should attempt to review the information on their page as dispassionately as possible. After they have spent some time looking at the page in this manner, they should answer the three questions and provide evidence to support their claims about themselves. Their evidence might, for example, take the form of images, quotations, or comments from others. When participants arrive for the session, have each person show his or her social networking page via the LCD projector and share his or her responses to the three questions.

Focus

Self-reflection and self-evaluation: With the proliferation of social networking sites, many people now feel free to make statements that they might not make during a face-to-face conversation. In fact, many people post content on the Web without evaluating how it might affect others or even what it might say about themselves. This activity offers participants the chance to evaluate their own social networking page in order to help them learn to see what others might see when visiting the page. As group members learn to look critically at their (and their friends') social networking pages, they begin to see themselves as others see them, and this revelation may or may not be encouraging.

Equipment

Computer with Internet connection, LCD projector

Users

10 to 15

Processing

Most of the processing for this activity consists of having individuals share their social networking pages and their answers to the three evaluation questions. If time allows, it is also useful to give other participants time for questions and comments regarding each person's page and his or her self-evaluation.

Go Wireless!

Most of the technology use for this activity occurs prior to the session, since participants must complete most of the activity on their own. When sharing their responses to the three questions, however, it is not necessary for participants to project their social networking pages on-screen; participants could bring printed copies to show to the group.

Upgrade

After participants have examined and critiqued their own social networking page, ask them to conduct a similar analysis of a close friend's page. The purpose here is to help participants see that who they are (in the eyes of others) consists not only of what they say and post on their own page but also of what is said about them on their friends' pages. Indeed, we can learn about ourselves by examining the company we keep. If, for example, all of my friends on a social networking site use crude language or make approving references to drugs or alcohol, then that says something about me. In this light, having your group members examine other social networking pages gives them a chance to see what others may think of them because of the friends they have.

Who Am I, Friend?

Overview

As evidenced by the time and effort put into creating and personalizing social networking pages, many people feel very proud of them. Sometimes, however, social networking sites increase a person's quantity of friendships even as the depth of his or her relationships suffers. This activity challenges your group members to improve the depth of their relationships with each other so that they can work more effectively and efficiently together. Specifically, the activity calls on participants to collect images and information from fellow group members' social networking pages in order to see how well they really know one another (or at least how well they know each other's social networking pages!).

Directions

Prior to the session, collect the following information from each participant's social networking page: one wall post currently on his or her front page, one musical favorite, one favorite book, one favorite TV show, one favorite movie, hometown, one picture, and one additional miscellaneous piece of information. If some participants do not have a social networking page, ask them to provide the same information via e-mail or in writing. Once you have collected this information from each participant, create a presentation that allows you to introduce the information in piecemeal

Who Am I, Friend? *(continued)*

fashion; for example, arrange the presentation so that each slide holds one piece of information. The various pieces of information should be presented in order from least obvious to most obvious. Create such a presentation for each person in the group.

Using presentation software, present the information one piece at a time. As you gradually disclose information about a given person, the rest of the participants should attempt to identify that person.

As participants attempt to identify a group member from information collected from his or her social networking site, participants gain an idea of how well they know each other.

Focus

Relationship depth: With the advent of social networking sites, the term *friend* has taken on new meanings. People can now have friends whom they have met in person only once—or not at all. Because of this change, it is important that people have opportunities to develop deeper understandings of and relationships with those they come into contact with. This activity tests group members' knowledge of one another and encourages them to develop deeper, more meaningful relationships.

Equipment

Computer with Internet connection, LCD projector

Users

10 to 15

Processing

- Who was the most difficult to identify? Why?
- Who was the easiest to identify? Why?
- How well do you know your fellow members in this group?
- How much of ourselves do we disclose online versus in person?
- Is it easier to disclose information about ourselves online or in person?
- What does it mean to have a relationship with someone in person?
- What does it mean to have a relationship with someone online?
- Is there a difference? Should there be?

- How do we develop substantive online relationships?
- How do we develop substantive in-person relationships?

Go Wireless!

Rather than present the information via an LCD projector, read the information to the group so that participants can attempt to identify each individual.

Upgrade

After the group has completed the activity, have participants pair up to interview and learn five new facts about each other (i.e., facts not presented on the person's social networking page).

Blog About It

Overview

This is an excellent activity on two levels. First, participants are asked to create a blog for your group, which is a great way for them to share information and express their thoughts and feelings about events and activities relevant to the group. Second, completing this activity helps your group members explore existing blogs on topics of interest to the group and begin to judge the credibility of those blogs.

Directions

Identify a blog that addresses a topic of interest to your group. For example, if your group consists of students who are interested in recreational therapy and the rights of people with disabilities, they might review a blog called The Howling Wolfe (http://thehowlingwolfe.blogspot.com/). You can find many more examples by doing a simple Google search for blogs on a particular topic of interest (e.g., use the search terms *blogs* and *disabilities*). Preview all blogs before sharing them with your group; once you have selected an appropriate blog, project its front page onto a screen and ask the group to offer thoughts and comments about the visible posts on the blog.

Blog About It *(continued)*

Focus

Part of this activity's focus depends on the specific blog selected. We recommend using blogs that are pertinent to your group and that invoke levels of investment and response that can lead to thoughtful conversations. Regardless of the blog topic, however, this activity gives you an opportunity to help participants practice honest sharing with one another. The session should be a time for people to feel comfortable sharing their thoughts and ideas regardless of whether they are in the majority or the minority. The activity also gives you a chance to address the widely varied reliability and credibility of information found via the Internet. With the evolution of blogs and even Twitter (a mini blogging and social networking service)—in addition to the various other kinds of material available on the World Wide Web—there is now a tremendous amount of information to evaluate for accuracy and reliability on any given topic. Blog About It gives you a platform for addressing these issues.

Equipment

Computer with Internet connection, LCD projector

Users

10 to 15

Processing

- What was the message of the blog entry?
- Do you personally agree with the author's view? Why or why not?
- Is the author believable? Why or why not?
- What is the whole group's level of agreement with the author?
- How would you craft a response to this blog entry?
- Did you feel comfortable sharing your thoughts and opinions? Why or why not?
- How did you help (or how could you have helped) others feel comfortable with sharing?
- How did others help (or how could they have helped) you feel comfortable with sharing?
- Why is it important to help people feel comfortable with sharing?

Go Wireless!

Bring printed copies of blog posts that you would like the group to discuss; in a way, this approach may even be easier to facilitate insofar as each participant has the blog content to read at his or her own pace.

Upgrade

Create (or have the participants create) a blog for the group. To get started, you might visit Blogger at www.blogger.com and follow the instructions for creating a blog. It's free and easy! The blog should represent the group and should express the group's consensus on the topic under consideration. Potential blog topics include the group's own current events, as well as general issues such as homelessness, social equality, political questions, and any other issues of interest to the group that are likely to generate active commenting.

Fact or Fiction

Overview

This activity emphasizes lessons from Blog About It that relate to the credibility and reliability of electronic sources. In this day of electronic access, where anyone can post anything online, it is vital to understand that not all information on the Internet is accurate or even well intended. In this activity, after searching for two facts and a lie on a given topic, small groups challenge one another to discern the lie from the facts. In doing so, participants start to realize that they may need to research information in detail before accepting it as fact.

Directions

Have participants form groups of three or four members each and assign each group a topic (or allow them to select their own). Topics might address a historical event or a popular figure (see figure 3.2 on p. 95 for examples). Ask each team to search the Web for two facts and one piece of false information about its topic, then share its results with the larger group. The other teams should attempt to discern the false statement from the truths.

Some of your group members may have very strong personal feelings regarding these topics, and in some cases, group members may find their identity in one or more of these issues. Because of this, it is very important to protect individuals in your group who may be disparaged by their connection to an unpopular topic or who may feel scared to indentify with one of the topics. To do this, we recommend revisiting the full value contract that you established with your group (see figure 1.1 on p. 11).

Fact or Fiction *(continued)*

Focus
Discernment: Attempting to separate good information from bad is a valuable skill, but doing so is particularly challenging in an age in which we are constantly bombarded by information from numerous, diverse, and often obscure or anonymous sources. This activity encourages participants to work together to separate fact from fiction.

Equipment
Computer with Internet access for each group

Users
Groups of 3 or 4

Processing
- Which was the hardest lie to identify? Why?
- Which was the easiest lie to identify? Why?
- Which were the hardest truths to identify? Why?
- Which were the easiest truths to identify? Why?
- How did you and your group work to determine what was true and what was false?
- What are some issues or situations where you have a hard time determining what is true and what is false? How did you discern the truth in such instances?
- How can you learn to better discern truth from falsehood?

Go Wireless!
Rather than having participants search the Web for information, have them present information about themselves. They should still select two truths and one lie, and the other group members then work to discern the lie from the truths.

Upgrade
To increase the difficulty of this activity, have each group come up with two lies and one truth. The rest of the activity remains the same.

Fact or Fiction

Subject

- Abortion
- Gay marriage
- Stem cell research
- Animal rights
- Cloning
- Nuclear weapons
- The environment
- Gay, lesbian, bisexual, and transgender issues
- Racism
- Cyber bullying
- Political corruption

Historical Event

- Fall of the Berlin Wall
- The Great Depression
- The Holocaust
- Sinking of the Titanic
- The (U.S.) Civil War
- The Vietnam War
- World War I
- World War II
- Assassination of John F. Kennedy
- Assassination of Martin Luther King Jr.

Popular Figure

- Britney Spears
- Lindsay Lohan
- Miley Cyrus
- Paris Hilton
- Zac Efron
- Usher
- 50 Cent
- Eminem
- Lil Wayne
- Green Day
- Metallica
- Guns N' Roses
- Sean Paul
- Beyoncé
- Kobe Bryant
- Michael Jordan
- Tiger Woods
- Brett Favre
- Peyton Manning
- LeBron James
- Barack Obama

Figure 3.2 Potential subjects for Fact or Fiction.

Crossing the Line

Overview

In this activity, you use current technology to poll your group and challenge participants to literally cross the line. The activity gives group members a chance to come closer together as they learn about one another and begin to recognize that every person in the group has his or her own opinions and experiences.

Directions

Create a Google form containing the following yes-or-no statements, e-mail the form to all participants, and instruct each participant to answer the questions. Using a Google form allows for anonymous responses and thus helps participants feel free to respond honestly. It also allows you to easily collect the responses and view them in the form of a chart.

- I brushed my teeth today.
- I did not take a shower this morning.
- I am a woman.
- I have black hair.
- I have blue eyes.
- I am left-handed.

Group members grow in understanding of one another by responding to survey questions via the Internet, and later in the group meeting, they respond to the questions by crossing a line.

Courtesy of Ross Eli Baylis

- I was not born in the United States.
- I have been out of the country.
- I was raised poor.
- I was not raised with both biological parents.
- I come from a working-class family.
- My parents did not receive a college degree.
- I was held back in school.
- I have a visible or invisible disability.
- I am gay or have a close family member or friend who is.
- I have been called fat.
- I have been discriminated against.
- I have discriminated against others.

To use Google Docs, you will need to create a Gmail account. Once you have created your account, visit http://docs.google.com and click the "New" button on the left-hand side of the screen. Then select "Form" from the drop-down menu and follow the on-screen prompts to create your online survey. When you have finished creating your survey instrument, click on the "Email this Form" button in the upper right-hand corner in order to send the survey to any number of people. Once you have created the form, e-mail it to all of your participants and ask them to complete it by a specific deadline. When all of your participants have responded to the statements, use the "Chart" option to print out the responses, along with the percentage of participants who responded positively and negatively to each statement.

At your next gathering, put a long piece of tape on the floor across the center of the room and ask participants to stand on either side of the tape (i.e., with about half of the group on each side of the tape). Instruct participants to remain silent throughout the entire activity, then tell them that you are going to read the statements that they responded to via e-mail and share with them the percentage of people who responded positively and negatively to each statement. After you have provided the group with the percentage responses for a given statement, ask participants to cross the line if they responded positively to the statement that you just read. For example, you might say, "Sixty-six percent of people in our group say they have been discriminated against. If you have ever been discriminated against, please cross the line." It is important to make clear to participants that there is no "positive" or "negative" side of the line. Group members should simply cross the line if they responded positively to the statement that was read. Individuals should take notice of who crosses the line

Crossing the Line *(continued)*

with them and who does not. Once those desiring to cross the line have done so, pause briefly, then read the next statement and its percentages. Proceed in this fashion through all of the statements.

Focus

Similarities and differences: People often feel that they are all alone or that no one understands what they are feeling. This activity encourages individuals to see both similarities and differences between members of the group. While the idea of crossing the line may be stressful because participants may feel that they will have to move alone, the act of moving and seeing others move as well can be a very powerful experience. Seeing other people cross the line with oneself can be empowering and freeing; it can even prompt a moment of realization: "I am not alone." This activity encourages participants to be honest and share their experiences with one another.

Equipment

E-mail addresses of participants, computer with printer and Internet access

Users

12 to 25

Processing

- Which statement was the funniest? Most embarrassing?
- Did you lie (intentionally or by accident) about any of the questions? If so, which one and why?
- Were you ever alone on one side of the line? If so, what did that feel like?
- Were you ever scared to cross the line? If so, when and why?
- Did you ever hesitate to go across? If so, when and why?
- Did you feel uncomfortable when you walked across? Why?
- Did you feel uncomfortable when you watched someone else walk across? If so, who and why?
- Did you feel better when someone else walked across with you? Why or why not?
- Do you think crossing the line at certain times changed other people's view of you? Why or why not?
- Are there lines in your life that you need to cross but are afraid to because of what people might think?
- What are you going to do with the feelings that this activity elicited in you?

Go Wireless!

Using the Google form allows group members to share anonymously and therefore encourages honesty, but the activity can be done simply by reading the statements and asking group members to cross the line when they are in agreement with the statement. If you do not have access to the technology but would like to retain the anonymity, you can distribute a printed form to participants and have them give their responses to you in writing prior to the session.

Upgrade

This activity is already an emotionally demanding experience. If your group is ready for an extra challenge, we recommend that you include more controversial statements (e.g., "Abortion is acceptable at any time during a pregnancy" or "Illegal aliens are destroying our country") that will increase the difficulty of crossing the line and intensify the group discussion after the activity. Another highly effective adaptation is to use statements that are specifically applicable to your group.

When addressing questions of this nature, it is possible that some group members may have had personal experiences directly related to the questions posed. In these cases, we would encourage you to be very sensitive if individuals wish to step out of this activity. To create a safe atmosphere for sharing, we recommend revisiting the full value contract that you established with your group (see figure 1.1 on p. 11). It is important to make sure that any additional questions are not intentionally offensive. Some questions may be perceived as offensive by the very nature of the question being asked, but care can be taken when phrasing questions related to difficult topics. Likewise, all questions selected should have particular relevance to the group as a whole and experiences the group has had or is likely to have.

Based on B. Heermann, 1997, *Building team spirit: Activities for inspiring and energizing teams* (New York: McGraw-Hill), 56-57.

Forward Legends

Overview

Forwarded e-mails clog our inboxes everyday. Some make us laugh, and others make us cry. Some cause us to pause and think about humanity, and others promise untold riches if we simply share a few pieces of personal information (e.g., our bank account or social security number).

Forward Legends *(continued)*

This activity uses several such e-mail forwards to challenge your group to explore not only the veracity of a given piece of e-mail but also what makes it believable to so many people. The upgrade for this activity asks participants to work together to search the Internet for the most recent forward legend that is filling people's inboxes.

Directions

Have the participants form teams of three or four members each and provide each team with two or three forwarded e-mail messages that urge the reader to take a certain action or respond to the sender in a certain way (see figure 3.3 on pp. 101-106 for examples). Ask each team to read each e-mail with an eye toward reasons that the e-mail should or should not be believed. Once the groups have created their lists of reasons, ask each team to share its findings with the larger group.

Focus

Discernment: Attempting to separate good information from bad is an extremely valuable skill, and it is made even more difficult when receiving e-mails from supposedly reliable sources. It is particularly hard for many people to discern what is true and what is false when the sender is intentionally attempting to fool the reader into taking a certain action. This activity encourages participants to work together in learning how to separate reliable information from attempts to deceive.

Equipment

Computer with Internet connection for each group

Users

Groups of 3 or 4

Processing

- What makes the e-mail message believable?
- What makes the message unbelievable?
- Is the message effective? Why or why not?
- How do you decide whether or not you should believe the content of a message?
- What are some clues that a message should not be believed?
- How can you determine whether or not a person in your group should be believed?
- How can others know that you are someone who can be believed?
- How can discernment skills help a group function better as a team?

Go Wireless!

Technology is not necessary for this activity. You will have all the supplies you need if you arrive with printouts of preselected forward legends or simply use the forward legends in figure 3.3.

Upgrade

Ask each group to search online for e-mail scams that seem effective, then have each group's members share with the larger group their views on why the chosen scams were particularly effective. End the session by having the entire group create a list of precautions to take when receiving unsolicited e-mails.

Sample 1

Dear Valued Customer:

We regret to inform you that your eBay account could be suspended if you don't re-update your account information. To resolve this problems please click here and re-enter your account information. If your problems could not be resolved your account will be suspended for a period of 24 hours, after this period your account will be terminated.

For the User Agreement, Section 9, we may immediately issue a warning, temporarily suspend, indefinitely suspend or terminate your membership and refuse to provide our services to you if we believe that your actions may cause financial loss or legal liability for you, our users or us. We may also take these actions if we are unable to verify or authenticate any information you provide to us.

Due to the suspension of this account, please be advised you are prohibited from using eBay in any way. This includes the registering of a new account. Please note that this suspension does not relieve you of your agreed-upon obligation to pay any fees you may owe to eBay.

Regards, Safeharbor Department eBay, Inc

The eBay team.

This is an automatic message. Please do not reply.

Figure 3.3   Five sample forward legends.

From B.D. Wolfe and C. Penton Sparkman, 2010, *Team-building activities for the digital age: Using technology to develop effective groups* (Champaign, IL: Human Kinetics).

Forward Legends *(continued)*

Sample 2

Subject: FW: PLEEEEEASE READ!!!! It was on the news!

Dear friends,

Something to share with all of u. Would u believe if this is true? Read on..... For those who need money badly and this is one opportunity to try it! I'm an attorney, and I know the law. This thing is for real. Rest assured AOL and Intel will follow through with their promises for fear of facing a multimillion-dollar class action suit similar to the one filed by PepsiCo against General Electric not too long ago.

> Dear Friends,
>
> Please do not take this for a junk letter. Bill Gates is sharing his fortune. If you ignore this you will repent later. Microsoft and AOL are now the largest Internet companies and in an effort to make sure that Internet Explorer remains the most widely used program, Microsoft and AOL are running an e-mail beta test. When you forward this e-mail to friends, Microsoft can and will track it (if you are a Microsoft Windows user) for a two week time period. For every person that you forward this e-mail to, Microsoft will pay you $245.00, for every person that you sent it to that forwards it on, Microsoft will pay you $243.00 and for every third person that receives it, you will be paid $241.00. Within two weeks, Microsoft will contact you for your address and then send you a cheque.
>
> Regards.
>
> Charles S. Bailey
> General Manager Field Operations

I thought this was a scam myself, but two weeks after receiving this e-mail and forwarding it on, Microsoft contacted me for my address and within days, I received a cheque for US$24,800.00. You need to respond before the beta testing is over. If anyone can afford this Bill Gates is the man. It's all marketing expense to him. Please forward this to as many people as possible.

Figure 3.3 *(continued)*

From B.D. Wolfe and C. Penton Sparkman, 2010, *Team-building activities for the digital age: Using technology to develop effective groups* (Champaign, IL: Human Kinetics).

Sample 3

Greetings,

Your email address was entered into our November Microsoft X-Box promotional competition by either yourself or a friend, or perhaps a family member, at http://www.prize-giveaway.com

This is a prize draw, you have actually won a brand new Microsoft X-Box 360 Gaming Console!

Your package also includes these top 5 games:

- Halo 3

- Gears of War

- Call of Duty: Modern Warfare 2

- Bioshock

- Mass Effect

You are now invited to login to our website and claim your prize that you have already won. There are only 9 winners in total this month, out of thousands of emails, so do count yourself lucky!

We have provided the following web link for you, it is temporary and expires in 72 hours. If you do not login within this time, your winning shall unfortunately be returned to the prize pool.

Here is your link!

[LINK REMOVED]

On this page you will need to enter this pass code number to proceed: [Code Removed]

This is very important. Do not lose that number! Put in your address, and we will send your X-Box 360 to you.

We hope that you will enjoy your new X-Box 360 gaming console.

Congratulations on winning,

From Microsoft and the Prize-Giveaway.com team!

Figure 3.3 *(continued)*

From B.D. Wolfe and C. Penton Sparkman, 2010, *Team-building activities for the digital age: Using technology to develop effective groups* (Champaign, IL: Human Kinetics).

Sample 4

Subject: Package deposited in your name here

This is an official notification of the availability of a package deposited in your name and it is not a sales solicitation or SPAM.

We are Diplomats that use our immunity and status to safekeep special and valuable packages and baggage in trust for reputable clients that are honest and trustworthy.

We work in collaboration with top firms and Governments of various countries as we have earned a name as a service whose hallmarks in reliability and confidentiality are revered.

International missions, Fellow Diplomats and Embassies of the world have used our services to satisfaction.

A benefactor whose identity can not be disclosed because of the Non Circumvention and Non Disclosure Agreement that was signed with the said benefactor when the packages were being deposited made you the beneficiary of a package containing some amount of money and stated clearly that you should only be contacted when the time signed for it to be in our care elapses and the time has already elapsed that is why you are being contacted.

The Non Circumvention and Non Disclosure Agreement signed with the benefactor mandates us to fully divulge and disclose the benefactor's identity 18 months after the beneficiary has received the funds.

The funds in the package is (Two Million, Seven Hundred Thousand U.S. Dollars) and we confirm that these funds are fully free of any liens, or encumbrances and are clean, clear and non-criminal origin and are available in the form of CASH.

You are hereby advised to send your Full Contact Information as well as the name of the closest airport to your city in the format stated below so that the funds would be brought to your Country of residence by 3 Diplomats who would accompany you to your bank (if you want them to) to deposit the funds in your name and submit all

Figure 3.3   *(continued)*

From B.D. Wolfe and C. Penton Sparkman, 2010, *Team-building activities for the digital age: Using technology to develop effective groups* (Champaign, IL: Human Kinetics).

documentations that has to do with the origin of the funds in other to exonerate you from any form of investigations or interrogation and to authenticate the fact that the funds are clean and has no links whatsover with either drugs or terrorism.

The Requested Information is to ensure that no mistake or error is made and it should be forwarded in the manner stated below:

Your Full Name: _____

Your Complete Address: _____

Name of City of Residence: _____

Name of Closest Airport to your city of Residence: _____

_____

Direct Telephone Number: _____

The Telephone number is very necessary because the number would be called by the Diplomats before the funds would be handed over to you so as to ensure that the package is handed over to the right person.

So, its mandatory you send your Direct Telephone Number preferably your Mobile or Cell Phone Number.

Complete the above and send back to me as soon as possible.

We are waiting for your response.

God be with you.

Mrs Kirsten Windus.

Figure 3.3 *(continued)*

From B.D. Wolfe and C. Penton Sparkman, 2010, *Team-building activities for the digital age: Using technology to develop effective groups* (Champaign, IL: Human Kinetics).

Sample 5

URGENT BUSINESS ASSISTANCE STRICTLY CONFIDENTIAL)

I am the manager of bills and exchange at the foriegn remittance department of the (ABN AMRO BANK AMSTERDAM). I am writting you this letter to ask for your co-operation to carry out this transaction. We discovered some abandoned sum $15,500,000(FIFTEEN MILLION, FIVE HUNDRED THOUSAND U.S DOLLAR) in an account that belongs to one of our foriegn customer who died along-side his entire family in a terrorist train bomb blast in Spain some few months ago. We have advertised for his next of kin to come forward to claim this money, but nobody came yet to apply for the claim.

To this effect,i and other official in my department have decided to look for a trusted foriegn partner who can stand in as the next of kin of the deceased as we cannot do it only ourselves and claim this money. We need a foreign partner to apply for the claim on our behalf because of the fact that the customer was a foreign and we don't want this money to go into the treasury as unclaimed fund.

Every document to effect this process will emanate from my table and i will perfect every document to be in accordance with the banking law and guideline,so you have nothing to worry about and we have agreed that 30% of this money will be for you,while 10%will be for any expenses incured on both sides wihile 60% will be for my colleagues and me. If you are willing to help us,please indicate by replying this letter and putting in your name, private telephone number,fax and permanent residential address via my private email address below.I awaits your immediate response to enable us start this transaction as soon as i recieved your reply,i will send you a text application form for immediate APPLICATIION OF CLAIM.

Please contact me even if you are not intrested in my proposal to you to enable us scout for another partner in the event of non-interest on your part. Thanks for your co-operation

Mr Piet Van Jan

Figure 3.3 *(continued)*

From B.D. Wolfe and C. Penton Sparkman, 2010, *Team-building activities for the digital age: Using technology to develop effective groups* (Champaign, IL: Human Kinetics).

Identity Theft

Overview

This is another activity that uses social networking sites to help participants explore issues related to relationships. In this case, participants bring information from their social networking pages and take on the role of someone else in the group based on the information provided from that person's page. One's identity is ever-changing: Who am I? Who do I want to be? Such questions can have a multitude of answers for young adults, and this activity helps you start a conversation about this rich topic with your group.

Directions

Prior to the session, print each participant's profile from his or her social networking page; then, as participants arrive for the session, give each person his or her printed profile page and a name tag to wear in a highly visible fashion. If any members of the group do not have a social networking profile, ask them to write the following information on a sheet of paper: favorite music groups, favorite books, favorite TV shows, favorite movies, hometown, and one additional miscellaneous piece of information about themselves.

Taking on the identity of other group members helps participants work on listening skills.

Once all participants have their profile pages and name tags, have them pair up and exchange profile pages with a person they do not know very well. Each person should select three interesting descriptors about his or her partner from the profile page; for clarification, the partners should briefly discuss these bits of information. Once the pairs have finished their discussions, each person should assume the identity of his or her partner and swap name tags with him or her. Do *not* swap printed profile pages—discard them at this time. Now, for example, Joe who likes pizza, plays soccer, and hails from Hawaii becomes Jane who plays trombone, scuba dives, and has five brothers—and vice versa.

Next, everyone pairs up with a different person (each participant will pair up with a total of three people during the game). So Joe, whose new identity is Jane, now meets a second person and tells her that his name is Jane and that he plays trombone, scuba dives, and has five brothers. His partner shares similarly about his or her own new identity. The partners should share the information with each other only once, which encourages participants to listen carefully the first time. Then these two partners swap identities with each other and move on to meet one more person with whom they will swap identities. Once the participants have each met three people, they keep the name tag they have ended up with.

At this point, ask everyone to stand in a large circle and have each person take a turn introducing himself or herself in his or her present identity; that is, each participant should share the name and three descriptors of the person whose name tag he or she currently possesses. Once this introduction is complete, the real owner of the name tag should come forward and confirm or correct the information just provided about him or her. The person who just shared then returns the name tag to its owner, and that person shares his or her current assumed identity. Continue this process until all participants have shared their identities.

Focus

Listening and identity: In a world filled with technology, the ability to listen is becoming rarer. In fact, we often just don't listen very well. We nod our heads and say "uh huh," but oftentimes we don't really hear. Technology has also changed the concepts of relationship and identity. People now have Facebook friends—people they have never met in person or, in some cases, even spoken with. This activity highlights the importance of listening and encourages participants to go beyond surface-level conversations. It also encourages participants to address questions related to their own identity. All of us who use social networking pages choose to share pieces of who we are through this medium, but do these descriptions give an accurate picture of who we are? Are we sharing ourselves or creating alter egos on our social networking pages?

Equipment

For each participant: printed social networking profile, name tag, marker pen

Users

10 to 20

Processing

- Who was most accurate in his or her identity theft? Least accurate?
- What did you learn about someone else?

- Why is it important to learn about those around you?
- How well do you really know the people around you? (Consider friends from social networking sites.)
- Did the facts shared about you correspond closely with the way you would like to be viewed? How so or how not?
- What did you learn about yourself?
- Describe a time when you have wanted to be someone else.
- How can we each embrace our own identity?

Go Wireless!

Instead of using social networking profiles, simply ask each participant to think of three distinctive facts about himself or herself. For example, a student might think of these three: I play the trombone, I like to scuba dive, and I have five brothers. To aid in the selection of facts, you could provide fill-in-the-blank statements for each person to complete, and participants' responses could then become the facts that they share. For example: I'm afraid of _____. I collect _____. I always _____. I never _____. My favorite place is _____. My favorite book is _____. I have _____ siblings. My favorite movie is _____. My favorite TV show is _____. My favorite song is _____.

Once all participants have determined the three characteristics they will share, ask participants to find someone they do not know well and proceed with the activity according to the original instructions.

Upgrade

You can easily increase the difficulty of this activity by increasing the number of facts that must be remembered or the number of people that each participant must meet. Additionally, once the activity is complete, rather than ask each person to identify herself or himself upon being described by his or her imposter, ask the group to guess who is being described based on the information provided. The rest of the rules remain the same.

Get an Earful

Overview

Young people seem to have no problem expressing themselves; however, their self-expressions are sometimes made by means of calculated images projected to certain audiences based on specific expectations.

Get an Earful *(continued)*

Participants in this activity respond to question prompts via voice messages, which can then be shared with the group; thus, the activity gives your participants a fresh way of expressing themselves in an environment where they are encouraged to be genuine.

Directions

Create an account at www.wiggio.com. Once you have your account, you will want to create a group. Click on the "Create New Group" link at the top of the page. Provide a group name, group password, group purpose, and group description, and click "Create." We recommend using a name that is representative of your group (e.g., Class of 2010 or English 101). Next you will need to invite all of your group members to join your newly created Wiggio group. Enter the e-mail addresses for each person, select how you would like them to receive information from the group (we recommend selecting "each post by email"), and provide a custom welcome message if desired.

Once the group has been formed, you will want to pose a question to the group members. To do this, click on the "Message" link in the top menu bar and select "Voice Note." Check the "Select Everyone" option in the Roster window (so that your question goes to all of the group members) and record your message. You can ask group members to respond to questions such as these:

- What is one asset you bring to the group?
- What do you hope to receive from participating in the group?
- What are your strengths?
- How do you relate to other people?

Participants in a group that has existed for some time might be asked questions that are more deeply revealing and thought provoking: Whom do you most admire? What is your view on immigration? How should our community deal with the issue of poverty? What do you think is the most important issue facing the United States today? Should the government bail out failing organizations such as banks and car manufacturers?

After you have sent your message, participants will receive an e-mail alerting them to the fact that there is a voice message for them to listen to. They can either download the message from their e-mail or visit the Wiggio site to hear the message. Ask participants to respond to the question in another voice note that is sent to all members of the group. (It is important to remind group members to click the "Select Everyone" option so that their response goes to everyone.)

We recommend allowing about a week for participants to leave their voicemail messages. Participants are also able to record more than one message if they think of additional ideas or would like to respond to another response. As with any activity, ask participants to be respectful and use inoffensive language in their responses. Also, ask participants to try to remember content from other team members' voice messages so that they can discuss it readily when the group reconvenes.

When the group reconvenes, log in to Wiggio and play selected responses through a computer with speakers and an Internet connection. The facilitator should screen the responses before the group reconvenes and select responses that might generate significant conversation but are also representative of all responses provided.

Focus

Self-exposure: Exposing who we really are can be an extremely difficult task; at the same time, some individuals feel comforted when they have the opportunity to expose some of their true self in a manner that is not face-to-face. For newly formed groups, this activity allows participants to learn more about one another in a relatively nonthreatening environment. For more established groups, the activity allows members to explore difficult topics in a manner that may be less invasive and therefore more comfortable for some participants.

Equipment

Computer with Internet connection, speakers

Users

8 to 12

Processing

- Which questions were easiest for you to answer? Why?
- Which questions were hardest for you to answer? Why?
- Which responses surprised you the most? Why?
- Which responses made you feel comfortable? Why?
- Which responses made you feel uncomfortable? Why?
- Which responses did you most agree with? Why?
- Which responses did you least agree with? Why?
- Do you find it easier to share via the Web or in person? Why?
- How does the selected medium for sharing change your level of comfort?

Get an Earful *(continued)*

- How does the selected medium for sharing change your level of honesty?
- How can we become more comfortable and honest in our sharing with one another?

Go Wireless!

Simply ask your group members to write down their responses to the question prompts. This approach still promotes self-exposure and offers the benefit of using an alternative (i.e., other than face-to-face) medium for communication. Once group members have written their responses, you can have them either read their own responses or read another person's responses (either anonymously or with the group member's name attached).

Upgrade

To increase the difficulty of this activity, simply change the questions that you ask. You can make the questions more debatable as the group progresses (e.g., What are your feelings about abortion? What are your feelings about gay marriage? Should torture be legal if it is used to collect information deemed vital to national security? If so, who gets to decide what *vital* means?). When addressing questions of this nature, it is possible that some group members may have had personal experiences directly related to the questions posed. In these cases, we would encourage you to allow your group members to share their stories with the rest of the group. To create a safe atmosphere for sharing, we recommend revisiting the full value contract that you established with your group (see figure 1.1 on p. 11).

You can also change the questions to reflect current hot topics in the news or have the participants themselves determine the questions. With either of these options, it is important to prepare or screen the questions to make sure that they are not intentionally offensive. Some questions may be perceived as offensive by the very nature of the question being asked, but care can be taken when phrasing questions related to difficult topics. Likewise, all questions selected should have particular relevance to the group as a whole and experiences the group has had or is likely to have.

ASCII Art

Overview

This activity encourages group members to see images and ideas from different perspectives. Participants are asked to create images using only keyboard keys, which requires them to see images in new ways and understand how to apply new techniques to the process of creating images. It is vital that groups be able not only to see but also to understand different perspectives, and the processing questions for this activity help your group explore critical issues in doing so.

Directions

Prior to the activity, ask your participants to search the Web for examples of ASCII art in order to get an idea of what they will be doing in this activity. When you begin the session itself, have participants form teams of three or four members each, then give each group a phrase or word to re-create using keyboard characters (*not* simply the letters that spell the phrase or word). See figure 3.4 for examples. Begin with very simple images or even symbols (or emoticons; see figure 3.5) and have the groups use a keyboard to re-create the images with keyboard characters. As groups complete each word or phrase, have them show their pictures to the group.

Figure 3.4 Sample phrases rendered as ASCII art.

ASCII Art *(continued)*

:)	Classic smile
:')	Happy crying
:(	Classic sad expression
:-o	Yawn
:-)	Smile
:D	Laughter
>:)	Evil grin
:B	Buck teeth
:-#	Mouth with braces
:@	Scream
:P	Tongue sticking out (silly)
>:@	Anger
:/ or :\	Indifference
:-O	Yell, surprise
;)	Winking smile
(:D	Gossip, blabbermouth
/:)	Raised eyebrow
8)	Cool
XD	Hard laugh
:-&	Tongue-tied

Figure 3.5 Sample emoticons.

Focus

Perspective: People sometimes lose their perspective. We get used to seeing objects in a certain way, from a certain angle, and when that angle or our situation changes we may have difficulty seeing and comprehending. This activity asks participants to view words and phrases from a different perspective than usual. The intent is to help participants learn to view situations and experiences from different perspectives so that they can experience growth. As we metaphorically learn to see from different angles, we can begin to expand our abilities to perceive, which can lead to both personal and group growth.

Equipment

Computer for each team, LCD projector

Users

Groups of 3 or 4

Processing

- Which phrase was the hardest to draw? Why?
- Which was the easiest to draw? Why?
- Did it help to have multiple eyes looking at the same image? Why or why not?
- What did your eyes bring to the development of the drawing?
- Could you see the image as it was developing? Why or why not?
- What enabled you to finally see the image?
- Metaphorically speaking, what "images" do you have difficulty seeing in real life (e.g., finishing college, getting a job, getting married)?
- How might you get help from those around you in seeing these "images" from a different perspective?

Go Wireless!

Rather than having teams use a keyboard, ask them to use a pencil and paper to re-create the words or phrases. You can ask them to re-create the same images and otherwise follow the same instructions as for the original version of the activity. The caveat here is that participants can draw only those marks found on a computer keyboard. For example, if asked to draw a smiley face, they could not simply draw ☺. Rather, they would have to draw :) (a colon and a close-parenthesis mark).

Upgrade

Rather than re-creating words and phrases, have the teams draw pictures using only letters and symbols from the keyboard. For some examples, see figure 3.6 on page 116. The same instructions and processing questions apply as for the original version of the activity. For additional image ideas, you can search online for the term "ASCII art."

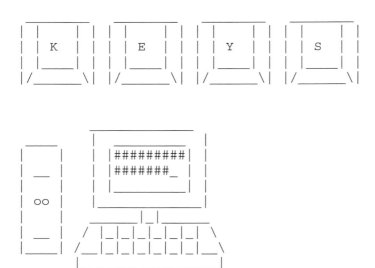

Figure 3.6 Computer keys and a desktop computer drawn by using only keyboard characters.

Texting Activities

I n the age of the text message, the power of the thumb has outgrown the power of the tongue. In general, young adults text more than they talk on their phones, but the speed at which text messages are entered and sent frequently leads to miscommunications—some humorous and others potentially disturbing or offensive. Just recently, I received a text from a student that said, "I thought it was at 'y10'." The student meant to say that she thought an exam was at 3:30, but her haste in entering and sending the message led to a miscommunication. We even hear stories these days from many students who lament that they have been "dumped" by a romantic partner via text message. Indeed, texting has become so second-nature to many people that they fail to think about the pitfalls involved in communicating this way. Yet if a team is to function and grow effectively, its members must be able to communicate clearly and sometimes quickly. Certainly, text messages are quick and convenient, and the activities presented in this chapter help users understand and meet the challenges that text messaging creates.

We anticipate that most participants will bring a working knowledge of text messaging and possess a cell phone that allows the user to send texts. One challenge that you may face, however, is the limited number of texts that some individual phone plans allow. Many students have unlimited texting, but some do not, and the texting activities presented here ask them to use some of their allotted texts. We encourage you to remind students of this consideration at the beginning of these activities and be sensitive to their perspective if they elect to save their texts. In such cases, you can partner people or allow them to work in small groups.

A second challenge—and perhaps a greater one—involves brushing up on your own texting skills! We encourage you to develop a clear understanding of how to use your cell phone to send text messages and then practice doing so.

For the activities using Twitter, you as the facilitator should go to www.twitter.com and set up a unique Twitter account for the activity. For example, the profile name to be used in an activity for a class might be called DrWolfeClass3940. Once you have established a unique profile, participants can use their own Twitter accounts to become followers of DrWolfeClass3940 for the duration of the exercise. Participants can use an account that they have already established or create a new one just for the group activity. For some of the activities presented here, participants may want to create user names that do not include their real names or allow them to be easily identified. A name like "SoccerFan" would be suitable and vague enough that others might not immediately know who the person is.

Participants whose cell phone plan allows unlimited text messaging can register via the Twitter site to have their "tweets" sent directly to their phone via text message. Participants whose phone includes a Web browser can use different applications (e.g., Tweetdeck, TwitterFon, Twitterific, and so on) to receive tweets from their phone.

As the facilitator, you will need to project a live feed of the activity's Twitter account. For example, the facilitator of DrWolfeClass3940 would connect a computer to the Internet and to an LCD projector, log on to the DrWolfeClass3940 account, and project the home page on a screen. You will also need to create what is called a hashtag for each activity. A hashtag is just a way of grouping related words or subjects by placing a # in front of the content name. It is best to create a hashtag unique to your group. For example, in the Tweelings activity, if the facilitator is a professor for a college course numbered 3940, he or she could create the hashtag #love/hate3940 and ask all participants to place #love/hate3940 in their responses to the questions for the activity.

This chapter contains the following activities:

Texting Gossip

Overview

Gossip can destroy any group. When participants start talking *about* one another rather than *with* one another, difficult times lie ahead. This activity weds the well-known telephone game with texting as your group members both text and whisper a message around the circle. The processing questions challenge participants to consider the problems and difficulties that come with texting; they also ask your group members to identify messages that they don't believe should be communicated via text message.

Directions

Prior to the activity, choose a phrase (with fewer than 300 characters) that has meaning to your group and translate it for text messaging (for help, visit http://transl8it.com/cgi-win/index.pl). Make sure that all participants have one another's cell phone numbers stored in their own phone's memory.

After arranging the group in a circle, text your message to the first person (it helps to have the message already loaded into your phone). The person who received the text then whispers the message to the next person in the circle. That person must then text the message to the next person. Continue in this fashion (i.e., alternating texts and whispers) until the last person receives the message via either text or whisper. The last person then verbally shares the message with the entire group.

Texting Gossip *(continued)*

Participants pass along a message by whispering and texting to other team members, which helps them learn how quickly miscommunication can take place.

Courtesy of Ross Eli Baylis

Focus

Communication: Some messages simply should not be communicated by electronic means ("I'm sorry; I just don't love you anymore"), yet people are increasingly doing so. This activity puts a 21st-century spin on an age-old favorite in order to demonstrate some of the difficulties inherent in communicating via text message. The difficulty will most likely begin in your own efforts to choose which messages to send; since many texts are limited to 300 characters, your choices are constrained right off the bat.

Equipment

Cell phone with text messaging capability for half of the participants in each group

Users

10 to 20

Processing

- What does the message mean?
- Why was the message chosen?
- Did the message break down? If so, where?

- How did you (personally) do in the activity?
- Did you use body language or facial expressions to help you communicate? How so?
- Were there any misinterpretations? If so, what led to them?
- Did breakdowns happen more often with whispers or with text messages? Why?
- How do we sometimes misinterpret messages we receive via text message?
- What can we take away from this exercise regarding communicating via text message?

Go Wireless!

Have participants form small groups of 8 to 10 members each and have each group stand in a straight line, with each person facing the back of another person. (This works best if the whole group can stand in line facing a chalkboard or whiteboard.) Provide a preselected picture to the last person in line (something simple, such as a stick figure drawing or simple drawing of a house). This person must then use his or her finger to sketch the image on the back of the person who is next in line. Then the person whose back was just drawn on draws the image on the back of the next person. This process continues until the image gets to the front of the line, whereupon the last person draws on the chalkboard or whiteboard what he or she felt so that the entire group can see the result.

Upgrade

To pose a greater challenge to your group, simply use a longer message or a more difficult drawing. For an additional upgrade, discuss the quotation the group used; in this case, of course, you should select the quotation purposefully with an eye toward topics that would be useful for your group to explore.

Speed-Texting

Overview

Communication is one of the keys to any group's success, yet it is also an area that most groups struggle with. Texting has moved communication into a whole new realm, and this activity uses a humorous form of relay race to help your group members become familiar with some of the difficulties inherent in communication generally and texting in particular.

Speed-Texting *(continued)*

Directions

Have participants form two equal teams and have each team stand in a straight line. Next, have the members of each team share their cell phone numbers with each other. Then, provide each team member (except the first person in each line) with a folded piece of paper on which is noted a simple task to complete. The participants should not look at the piece of paper until they are told to do so. To begin the activity, send a text message to the first person in line for each team. The message should read, "Text 'Bark like a dog' to the next person in your line." When the second team member receives the message and barks like a dog, he or she can open his or her piece of paper, which indicates the next text to send. This second text message should read, "Hug the person who just texted you." Once the third person in line completes that task, he or she can then read his or her slip of paper and send the next text message. Continue in this fashion until one team has finished its relay. Figure 4.1 offers 15 sample text messages, thus enabling you to conduct this activity with as many as 30 participants without creating any additional text messages.

Focus

Communication: Text messaging has become a commonplace activity, but text messages are not always the best way to communicate. Unfortunately, many young people have yet to realize the pitfalls of texting, and they elect to use text messages when a phone call or even a face-to-face conversation would work better. This activity takes a humorous and competitive look at the information that people text to one another and the speed at which some people are able to text.

Equipment

Cell phone with texting capabilities for each participant, papers with written instructions (see figure 4.1)

Users

20 to 30

Processing

- Who was the fastest texter on your team?
- Who was the slowest texter on your team?
- Was there any miscommunication on your team? If so, why?
- How effective were you at passing the message?
- What would have improved your communication?
- What are some pitfalls in communicating via text?
- What are some benefits of communicating via text?

- Have you personally had any particularly positive or negative experiences when trying to communicate via text?
- How can you avoid misunderstandings when texting is the primary avenue of communication?
- What are some messages that might be best conveyed via text message?
- What are some messages that might not be best conveyed via text message?

Go Wireless!

Rather than having participants text instructions to one another, have them perform actions indicated by drawings on pieces of paper that you provide for them. Each person can view his or her instructions when the preceding person in line has completed his or her own task. This version of the activity allows participants to interpret the image, then complete the intended action. For instance, rather than texting "Bark like a dog," provide a piece of paper with a picture of a dog barking. The participant would open the piece of paper, interpret the action, and complete the action before the next person in line could open his or her piece of paper.

Upgrade

If time is not an issue, adapt the tasks to your particular group. For example, participants could receive text instructions to perform random

- Bark like a dog.
- Hug the person who just texted you.
- Hop on one foot five times.
- High-five the last person in your line.
- Sing "row, row, row your boat."
- Shake the hand of one person on the other team.
- Pat your head and rub your stomach for five seconds.
- Run around your entire group once.
- Play rock-paper-scissors with one person until you win once.
- Do five jumping jacks.
- Do five push-ups.
- Run around the other team once.
- Shout your name as loudly as you can.
- Shout "I love this game."
- Run to the front of the line and say "Finished."

Figure 4.1 Sample text messages for a group of 15.

Speed-Texting *(continued)*

acts of kindness for strangers or provide some form of service to others, such as picking up 10 pieces of litter or helping someone move a heavy package. In addition, texted messages could be intentionally ambiguous (e.g., "Find a man eating plant," which could mean either a man eating a plant or a plant that eats flesh) so that the individuals can interpret the message in their own unique way.

Text Alike

Overview

This activity uses texting to help participants see how they may (or may not) think alike and how some of their thinking may prove to be limiting. By asking group members to select famous people to fit into certain categories, your group will take a humorous look at some of the more colorful characters who grace the pages of gossip blogs and newspapers. The processing questions, however, challenge group members to examine the problems inherent in pigeonholing people and to recognize how that type of thinking can be detrimental to your group and its progress.

Directions

This activity requires that the facilitator be helped by an assistant or co-facilitator.

To begin the activity, ask group members to identify a famous person who matches a provided category. For example:

- Diva
- Football player
- Basketball player
- Golfer
- Tennis player
- NASCAR driver
- Bad actor
- Good actor
- Pop star
- Reality star
- Reliable news source
- Great American leader
- Well-known hero
- Dirty politician

- Religious leader
- Untrustworthy occupation
- Metrosexual
- Comedian
- Honorable occupation
- Group of people who face the most racial discrimination in the United States
- Offensive radio talk show host
- Angry white man
- Angry black man
- Person with a disability
- America's greatest challenge

For each category, everyone in the group should text a name to the phone of the facilitator's assistant, who types all of the responses into a document that can be shared. (This approach allows individuals to provide honest responses to the categories with some measure of confidentiality.) With some of these responses (e.g., group of people who face the most racial discrimination in the United States) participants may feel more comfortable with confidential responses. Additionally, with confidential responses, participants may be more likely to offer their true thoughts on each of the items. Once all responses have been recorded, share the results with the group by projecting the list of responses onto a screen via an LCD projector. We recommend creating a PowerPoint presentation in which the responses to each category are represented by a graph on a slide.

Focus

Labeling: Every person labels or makes judgments about other people without knowing them. We look at someone and assume, on the basis of some characteristic (e.g., gender, race, age, hair color, clothing style), that we know what that person thinks and how he or she will respond in a given situation. By asking your participants to fit individuals into particular categories, you are asking them to label or put an individual in a box—something that is done all the time but is not beneficial. This activity allows participants to see some of the problems with making assumptions and labeling people, and the processing questions encourage them to reflect on instances in which they themselves have been limited or held back by the labels people have placed on them.

Text Alike *(continued)*

Equipment

Cell phone with texting capabilities for each participant, computer, LCD projector

Users

10 to 12 (more participants would overload the co-facilitator, thus making it very difficult to tabulate responses)

Processing

- Which category generated the highest number of similar responses? Why?
- Which category generated the fewest similar responses? Why?
- Did any of the responses surprise you? Why or why not?
- Is there any question where you might have given a different response if the activity were not confidential? Why or why not?
- What does it say about us that we were able to find people that we thought belonged in these categories?
- What does it say about the people whom we selected for the specific categories?
- How can we resist putting people in boxes and categorizing them in limiting ways?
- How can we keep ourselves from being placed in boxes and being categorized in limiting ways?
- How do we overcome labeling (whether it is you or someone else being labeled)?

Go Wireless!

Rather than using text messaging, have participants write their responses on a piece of paper that they simply hand to the assistant. Results can be tabulated on paper and shared with the group.

Upgrade

Rather than using the provided categories (or others that focus on people outside of your group), develop categories that require participants to use group members in their responses. For example, you could include the categories athletic, dramatic, technologically savvy, and so on to fit the people in your group. In selecting the categories, it will be important to make sure that you have group members that could actually fit into the identified categories.

DbT (Death by Text)

Overview

For a group to be successful, it is vital that members be observant and able to remember important details. This activity offers a twist on a favorite party game that puts group members on the lookout for the "killer." As participants text messages to one another, they are called on to be more observant and to pay more attention to small details than they may have done in the past. Using this framework, the processing questions challenge your group members to identify times and situations where they could be more observant and pay more attention.

Directions

Prior to the start of this activity, make sure that each group member has all fellow members' cell phone numbers stored in his or her own phone. The game can be played while a group is engaged in other activities that would not be undercut by an occasional distraction. For example, if the group is meeting for several hours to do team-building or planning work, this activity could be done throughout the event. Explain to participants that they are going to be playing this game for about 3 or 4 hours (or the planned

Participants hone their observation skills by trying to identify the team member who is taking out other team members via text message.

DbT (Death by Text) *(continued)*

length of time for the primary activity they will be engaged in). Identify one person to be the killer (no one else should know who this individual is). During the agreed-upon game time (while the other activity is occurring), this person texts the letters "DbT" to other people in the group. A person who receives such a text must in some way identify himself or herself as figuratively "dead" to the whole group. For example, you might instruct participants to yell "Dead!" if they receive that message. When a person receives the message, he or she is out of the current round. The object is for everyone else to guess who the killer is before they are categorized as dead. To guess who the killer is, one group member must say, "I know who the killer is. Will anyone support me?" If no one is willing to be a witness for the accuser (without conversing about who they both believe is the killer), the game continues. If someone is willing to support the accuser, then the accuser may offer a name. If the accuser is correct, that round is over. If the accuser is incorrect, then both the accuser and the witness are out. The game continues either until the agreed-upon length of time has elapsed or an accuser (with the support of a witness) identifies the killer. Potential accusers should be alert to nonverbal communication from other group members and should especially look for signs of texting right before someone declares that he or she is now "dead."

Focus

Observation and memory: We have all been guilty of forgetting some-thing—even something very important—and we could all stand to improve our powers of observation. We tend to get involved in the activity of the moment and forget to properly attend to other important tasks. Sometimes we even get so involved in a task that we forget we are involved in other tasks at all. Because we live in a world where everything is only a mouse click away, we forget to remember! This activity encourages participants to hone their observation skills by remaining alert to a game while they are participating in another activity. It challenges both their memory skills and their powers of observation as they try to watch other members' nonverbal cues and notice if a team member has been texting just before another person declares that he or she is "dead."

Equipment

Each participant's cell phone with all fellow group members' cell numbers loaded into memory

Users

10 to 20

Processing

- Did you figure out who was the killer? If so, how?
- Did you ever forget that you were playing the game?
- What did it take for you to remember that you were playing the game?
- Did you care about playing the game while you were completing the other task? Why or why not?
- What tasks in life do you sometimes forget to do?
- How can you become better at remembering what is important?
- How can you become better at observing your surroundings (not just physical but also emotional)?

Go Wireless!

The wireless version of this activity requires reserving a dedicated time to play the game (rather than playing it during another activity). Ask the group to sit together in a circle. As before, identify one person to be the "killer" (other group members should not know who this person is). Rather than sending texts, the killer winks at a person to indicate that he or she is now "dead." The rest of the game proceeds as indicated in the instructions for the original version.

Upgrade

The upgrade combines the original and wireless versions. As in the wireless version, have the participants sit together in a circle (but this time around a table) with their cell phones in their laps. The killer texts the letters "DbT" to various participants, and the rest of the rules remain the same as in the original version, but with the increased difficulty that the killer must text as subtly as possible in order to avoid being seen. Even so, if everyone is looking at their cell phones to see if they have received a message, it can be very difficult to identify the killer.

Trailing the Text

Overview

This activity promotes teamwork and creativity through a technology-driven scavenger hunt. By providing clues via text message, you give your participants a chance to work together as they interpret clues and locate the next stop on their hunt. Participants also engage their creative side

Trailing the Text *(continued)*

by taking pictures throughout their journey. The processing questions challenge your group members to think about how they worked together, then apply those strategies in their regular work as a group.

Directions

Before the session begins, create 6 to 10 clues for activities that team members will have to complete (see figure 4.2 on p. 133 for ideas). Go to a texting translator site (such as http://transl8it.com/cgi-win/index.pl) and translate your clues into text messages with fewer than 300 characters.

To begin the session itself, have participants form small teams of four to six members each; make sure that each team designates one phone as the group phone and has at least one camera phone or digital camera among its members. Begin the activity by texting the first clue to one group, texting the second clue to the second group, texting the third clue to the third group, and so on, until all groups have received a clue. The order of the clues is not important. What matters is making sure that each group goes to a different first location. The groups then disperse from your meeting location and look for the location designated by their first clue. When a group arrives at its targeted location, its members should look for the answer to the question contained in their clue and take a picture. The picture should be the team's interpretation of the words that are rendered in all-capital letters in the text message. (In the examples provided, the relevant phrases are BEDHEAD, THE INCREDIBLE SHRINKING TEAM, BLESSING IN DISGUISE, HOLLYWOOD LOOK-ALIKE, RE-CREATE A SCENE FROM YOUR FAVORITE CHILDREN'S STORY, SINK OR SWIM, and THE SCENE OF THE CRIME.)

Once the group's members have discovered the answer and taken their picture, they can text both the photo and the answer to the facilitator. The facilitator will then respond with the next clue. (Team 1 would get the second clue, team 2 would get the third clue, and so on.) As the groups submit their photos, create a visual presentation that allows for whole-group viewing of the images once all groups have returned. We recommend creating a PowerPoint presentation wherein pictures are shown according to categories. When the group returns, begin the processing phase of the activity by showing all of the pictures submitted by the groups.

Make sure to test all of the cell phones you are using for each team before you begin the activity. Many cell phones will not receive text messages that contain more than 300 characters, so you should keep your messages below this limit. The activity can be done in a variety of locations—for example, on a campus, in a neighborhood, or in a certain area of a city. It works best if you use an area limited to a reasonable walking

Sending Instant Messages

For the Trailing the Text activity, you will need to send specific text messages to groups as they discover clues. You can do so most easily by using a computer to send your text messages to the various team phones. To use AOL Instant Messenger (AIM) to send and receive text messages from a computer, download the latest version of it to your PC or Mac. For Mac users who prefer to use the IM software installed on their computer, iChat works exactly like AIM and can be used instead.

Once you have installed the application, you can follow the following steps to send a message:

PC Users

1. Click the "People > Send an Instant Message" option.
2. In the "To" box, type +1 followed by the area code and phone number to which you want to send a text message. For example: +15555551234
3. Click the "Send" command.
4. The receiver can reply to the text via his or her cell phone. You will see the reply in the display window and can reply and chat.

Mac Users

1. Open iChat.
2. Click the "File > New Chat with Person" option.
3. In the "To" box, type +1 followed by the area code and phone number to which you want to text. For example: +15555551234
4. Click the "Send" command.
5. The receiver can reply to the text via his or her cell phone. You will see the reply in the display window and can reply and chat.

Please be aware that most national cell phone carriers work with AIM and iChat, but some regional carriers do not. Before doing the activity, be sure that the phone to which you are texting receives text messages via AIM and allows the user to reply to the messages.

Trailing the Text (*continued*)

distance (i.e., a few blocks at most) yet large enough that teams will not stumble over one another.

While it is possible for one facilitator to manage this activity from his or her cell phone, we recommend using a co-facilitator (or even a separate co-facilitator for each group). The activity can also be made easier if you use an instant messaging service, which allows you and any co-facilitators to send the text messages from a computer to the participants' cell phones. Participants can respond from their phones to the computer via instant messaging services that are compatible with many phones (e.g., AIM; see p. 131).

Focus

Teamwork and creativity: This activity requires an immense amount of teamwork within the smaller teams. It gives participants an opportunity to learn to work together and think creatively as a team—both of which are often difficult for many people—while learning about a location that they may be unfamiliar with.

Equipment

Cell phone with camera for each group and each facilitator, computer with Internet connection (and instant messaging service if desired), LCD projector

Users

Groups of 4 to 6

Processing

- What photos did you find funniest or most creative? Why?
- How did different groups interpret the pictures differently?
- What did you learn about the area today?
- What did you learn about your group members today?
- What did your teammates contribute to the process?
- What did you as a teammate contribute to the process?
- Would this activity have been easier with more people on your team? Why or why not?
- Would this have been easier with fewer people on your team? Why or why not?
- What can you learn from this activity about working with other people?
- What can you learn from this activity about being creative?

Go Wireless!

Rather than texting the clues, provide all of the clues to each team at the beginning of the activity. Stagger the groups' first clues, so that each team begins in a different place. Once a group arrives at a given location, its members will address a question that can be answered only from information found at that location. The group proceeds in this fashion through all of its clues and returns to the starting point upon completing the list. Once all groups have returned, you can start the processing phase by having each group share its answers to the questions. Rather than talking about how the groups interpreted the pictures, the processing could continue with the questions regarding teamwork.

Upgrade

You can easily upgrade this activity by increasing the difficulty of the clues and the questions that have to be answered at the various locations. These adaptations are particularly useful if your participants already know the area.

Text Message Scavenger Hunt

Clue	Text version of clue	Location to which the clue leads	Answer to question in clue (correct answer earns next clue)
If you decide you'd like another roommate instead, be sure to go here but not with **BEDHEAD**! For next clue, the person this building was named for was a dedicated what?	f U Dcide youd llk NothA room8 insted, b suR 2 go hEr bt not w **BEDHEAD**! 4 NXT clue, d prsn DIS bILdN wz named 4 wz a dedicated wt?	Residence life office on a college campus	Teacher
Oh, no! Your team has caught a rare virus called **THE INCREDIBLE SHRINKING TEAM**. You need to go here to find some healing cream. For next clue, text the fall/spring hours of operation.	Oh, n! yor team hz caught a rare virus caLd **d NcreDbL SHRINKING TEAM**. U nEd 2 go hEr 2 find som healing cream. 4 NXT clue, txt d fall/spring hrz of operation.	Health clinic on a college campus	M-W 8am-5pm; Th 9am-5pm; F 8am-4:30pm

Figure 4.2 Sample clues for Trailing the Text.

Clue	Text version of clue	Location to which the clue leads	Answer to question in clue (correct answer earns next clue)
Students, for you to work hard would be very wise; you may go here to pick up a check and find a **BLESSING IN DISGUISE**. For next clue, text the number of columns you see when you find your location.	Students, 4 U 2 wrk hard wud b v wise; U mA go hEr 2 pik ^ a chek & find a **BLESSING n DISGUISE**. 4 NXT clue, txt d # of coluMz U c wen U find yor location.	Financial aid building on a college campus (Use an actor dressed as a priest at this location so participants can take a photograph with the priest— "Blessing in disguise.")	8 columns
During orientation you sat in here before the frenzy; take a picture today with a **HOLLYWOOD LOOK-ALIKE** (it doesn't have to be just Paris or Lindsay). For next clue, text the name of the college when this building was built in 1929.	durN orientation U sat n hEr b4 d frenzy; tAk a pictuR 2day w a **HOLLYWOOD LOOK-ALIKE** (it doesnt hav 2 b jst Paris o Lindsay). 4 NXT clue, txt d nAm of d college wen DIS blLdN wz built n 1929.	Auditorium on a college campus	State Teacher's College
Reading, writing, the sound of mouse clicks . . . grab a Mocha to get your fix! From *Charlotte's Web* to Tinker Bell, this is the place where your imagination can swell! **RE-CREATE A SCENE FROM YOUR FAVORITE CHILDREN'S STORY**. For next clue, text the name of this location.	rEDN, writiN, d swNd of :0~ clikz . . . grab a Mocha 2 git yor fix! frm charliz Web 2 Tinker bell, DIS iz d plAc whr yor imagination cn swell! **RE-CREATE A SCENE frm yor FAVORITE chldrn'S STORY**. 4 NXT clue, txt d nAm of DIS location.	Campus library	Campus library

Figure 4.2 *(continued)*

Clue	Text version of clue	Location to which the clue leads	Answer to question in clue (correct answer earns next clue)
Here's where your team could **SINK OR SWIM**; go 3 times a week to avoid the freshman 15 whether you are a her or him! For next clue, text the year of dedication.	hErz whr yor team c%d **SINK o SWIM**; go 3 tImz a wk 2 avoid d freshman 15 wethR U R a her o him! 4 NXT clue, txt d yr. of dedication.	Campus recreation center	2000
Let's hope this is a place where you never spend any time, or happen to see **THE SCENE OF THE CRIME**. For next clue, text the number of steps leading to the entrance.	letz hOp DIS iz a plAc whr U nevr spNd NE tym, o hpn 2 c **d SCENE OF d CRIME**. 4 NXT clue txt d # of steps lEdN 2 d entrance.	Campus police station	20 steps

Figure 4.2 *(continued)*

Trivia Text

Overview

This activity not only requires everyone in the group to work together; it also helps participants recognize roles that they may have played during the activity. When playing a trivia game, there often seem to be some players who know it all and others who just don't know any of the answers. Even so, anyone can participate in conversations conducted during the deliberation period of this activity, and these conversations can help the group answer questions correctly. In any group, each person must have a role and must understand and embrace that role. This activity uses trivia to help demonstrate the importance of having, knowing, and embracing one's role rather than just "checking out" and being left out of the solution-finding process.

Trivia Text *(continued)*

Directions

Prior to the activity, gather 10 trivia questions from a Web site such as www.triviaplaying.com.

Once the group arrives, have participants form teams of three or four members each and make sure that someone in each group has unlimited texting service for his or her cell phone. You should also have a cell phone and should share your number with the participants. Begin the activity by stating or showing on a screen the first trivia question. Each group's members should consult with each other to generate an answer, then text their response to the facilitator's cell phone. The first team to text the correct answer receives 1 point. Continue this process until all questions have been asked and answered.

Note: Scoring should be a secondary concern during this activity; the real focus is not on which team wins but on discovering and becoming comfortable with participants' roles within the group.

Focus

Teamwork and group roles: This activity requires participants to work together to generate answers to some potentially obscure trivia questions. In such situations, individuals typically find themselves in one of two categories: knowing all of the answers or knowing none of the answers. For those who know all (or many) of the answers, this activity can be particularly enjoyable, but those who don't know many of the answers may find themselves bored and frustrated. Both types (and any in between!) should be given a chance to share their thoughts and feelings at the end of the activity. The intent is for individuals to begin to identify their roles within the existing group, with the hope of becoming comfortable with those roles. Groups cannot function successfully if everyone has the same role (e.g., if we all act as the recorders of information or all send out reminders of the next meeting). Identifying roles is an efficient way for groups to operate; in many cases, however, group roles are left undefined, which results in confusion and frustration. This activity can be used to help team members discuss the importance of roles and learn to appreciate the different strengths that everyone brings to the group.

Equipment

Cell phone for each group and one for the facilitator

Users

Groups of 3 or 4

Processing

- Which question was the hardest?
- Which question was the easiest?
- Who knew the most answers?
- Who knew the fewest answers?
- How would you describe your role during this activity?
- Is that the role that you wanted to have, or is there another role that you would have preferred?
- How would you describe your role within this group more generally?
- Is this the role that you want to have, or is there another role that you would prefer?
- How can you further develop and become comfortable with your role in this group?
- How can we help each other in this process?

Go Wireless!

This activity can easily be completed without the use of cell phones. You can simply state the questions out loud, and group members can stand or raise their hands to signify that they have come up with an answer. The remainder of the instructions remain the same as for the original version.

Upgrade

To increase both the meaningfulness and the difficulty of this activity, select trivia questions related to the group or to a recent group activity. For example, if the group is based at a university, ask questions about the campus or the school fight song. Or, if the group has just completed a project or a trip, ask questions about that event. Personalizing the trivia questions will make the activity have more meaning for your group because the questions are directly related to a topic of interest or importance to the group members. Similarly, the difficulty of the activity can be increased because you can expect your group members to have a rudimentary knowledge of group-related experiences or events; therefore, you may ask more difficult trivia questions.

Hardware Hunt

Overview

This activity teaches the concept of reciprocity by having participants work together to find different pieces of technology. As participants rely on one another to find as many items as possible, they are challenged to use the strengths of everyone in their group—not just the people with whom they typically interact. The processing questions for this activity lay the ground work for each group member to see how he or she offers a unique skill or attribute to the group.

Directions

This activity requires that the facilitator be helped by an assistant or co-facilitator.

Have participants form teams of three or four members each and inform them that you are going to show them a list of items for them to locate. They may use only the items that they currently have with them, and their goal is to accumulate as high a team score as possible by locating as many items as they can. Whichever group has the most of a certain listed item (e.g., cell phones) gets 1 point. We recommend creating a Power-Point presentation wherein the listed items are displayed all at once so that groups can begin working collectively to locate the items. Allow 5 minutes for participants to complete this task. All items must be present in order to be counted (i.e., simply owning an item does not count—it must be on hand).

In order for items to be counted, participants must send a text message (or multiple text messages) identifying the number of each of the listed items to the phone of the facilitator's assistant, who types all of the responses into a document that can be shared. Whether participants elect to send one text message at the end of the time or multiple text messages throughout the activity is at the discretion of each group. However, participants should be informed that after 5 minutes they will not be able to submit any additional information. As the information is texted to the assistant, he or she should create an electronic document that shows the number of each item for each group. At the end of the activity, project the results on a screen. Have the participants determine which team has the most of each of the following:

- Cell phones
- MP3 players (OK to count cell phones with MP3 players)
- Contacts stored in cell phones
- Songs stored in MP3 players

- Audiobooks
- Earphones
- Ringtones
- Digital cameras
- Digital pictures stored on cameras or cell phones
- Calendar appointments for the upcoming month
- Games
- Movies
- Unopened e-mails
- Saved voicemails
- Text messages sent within the last 24 hours

Participants become aware of what they each bring to the group by collecting different pieces of technology.

Courtesy of Ross Eli Baylis

Note: Scoring is only a secondary concern during this activity because the true focus is not on which team wins but on learning to become interdependent with others.

Focus

Reciprocity: Reciprocity involves some level of interdependence on others. Indeed, life is about reciprocity. We cannot survive on our own; we need other people's help. In this activity, participants are asked to find certain objects within their group. If this were an individual activity, the final individual tallies would be much lower than the final group tallies will be. It is important to learn both how to help those who have less than we do and how to accept help from those who have more than we do. In this activity, even if one individual does not have much to offer in terms of gadgets, he or she likely still has *something* to offer, and he or she will in turn benefit from the rest of the group. Thus this activity offers participants an opportunity to explore reciprocity in a fun, nonthreatening way.

Equipment

Technology in participants' possession, one cell phone per group, one cell phone for the facilitator, computer, and LCD projector

Users

Groups of 4 to 6

Hardware Hunt *(continued)*

Processing
Processing for this activity begins with a review of the number of appropriate items possessed by each group.

- Who offered the most in your group?
- Who offered the least in your group?
- Does it matter who offered the most or the least? Why or why not?
- What does *reciprocity* mean?
- Is reciprocity important? Why or why not?
- When have you offered much to a group?
- When have you offered little to a group?
- How can we learn to both give assistance to others and accept assistance from them?

Go Wireless!
Rather than focusing on high-tech items, have participants search for other items, such as the following:

- Discover credit card
- Fingernail file
- Spearmint gum
- Pocketknife
- Ford car key
- Business card
- Gift card
- US $20 bill
- Lyrics to the *Brady Bunch* theme song
- Chewed pen cap
- Bobby pin
- Lip balm
- Bottle opener
- USB flash drive
- Driver's license
- Motorola RAZR cell phone
- One photo of five people
- US$1 in dimes
- The answer to the following equation $137 \times 17 + (83 \div 3) - 251$

Rather than have the groups text the number of items they possess, simply have them tally their items and verbally report their score before the 5-minute deadline.

Upgrade

Specify more precisely the type of hardware to locate. For example, rather than simply asking for a cell phone, require that it be an iPhone. Likewise, rather than just counting the number of stored voicemails, have participants count the number of stored voicemails from mothers. Here is a list of suggested changes:

- iPhones
- Red MP3 players (OK to count cell phones with MP3 players)
- Cell phone contacts beginning with the letter C
- Love songs stored in MP3 players
- Mystery audiobooks
- White earphones
- Ringtones featuring a cartoon character
- Ultra compact (i.e., pocket-size) digital cameras
- Digital pictures of people playing sports stored on cameras or cell phones
- Job-related appointments for the upcoming month
- Sudoku
- Cartoon movies
- E-mails from a significant other
- Saved voicemails from your mom
- Text messages sent within the last 3 hours

T9 Twist

Overview

For those who don't use predictive texting, this activity will prove particularly difficult and useful. T9 Twist (*T9* stands for "texting on 9 keys") uses the predictive texting feature found on many cell phones. Rather than requiring the user to completely spell each word—which can be laborious since each number button on the keypad corresponds to three letters of the alphabet—phones equipped with predictive texting offer options for

T9 Twist *(continued)*

automatically completing the word you are typing by predicting the most likely word based on the numbers you are pressing. While it may sound difficult, it is in fact fast and easy, and almost every person who texts with any regularity will understand and be proficient at predictive texting. The T9 Twist activity uses mixed-up sentences to help your group learn lessons related to some of the difficulties communicating via text message.

Directions

Have participants form teams of three or four members each and have each team designate an official cell phone. Make sure that you have a cell phone with strong reception and that each group has your cell phone number. You will then project mixed-up sentences, one at a time, onto a large screen. We recommend creating a PowerPoint presentation in which one slide contains the mixed-up sentence and the next slide provides the solution. Each sentence consists of words created via predictive texting, but they are not the correct words for the intended message. For example, if you type the number combination "6-3" in predictive texting, the phone displays the word *of*. However, 6-3 is also the combination for the word *me*, and frequent texters will easily recognize the substituted word. Each group must follow this decoding process to identify the correct words and thus make sense of the sentence.

Begin by showing the following example on the screen: "Ball of." Then ask the groups to text you their guess of the intended message. In this case, the answer is "Call me." Once the coded sentence appears on the screen, teams race to see who can first send the correct text message to the facilitator's cell phone. Figure 4.3 provides 10 sample sentences.

Focus

Communication: Text messaging has become a commonplace activity, but text messages are not always the best way to communicate, and, as can be seen from these mixed-up sentences, communication errors can abound when we use text messages. If a team is to work together effectively, its members must be able to communicate clearly, and (as with Speed-Texting) this activity takes another humorous and competitive look at the information people text to one another and how that information can be miscommunicated. Participants will gain awareness of how messages can be garbled and how to take care when communicating information via text message.

Equipment

Cell phone with texting capabilities for each team, computer, LCD projector

Users

Groups of 3 or 4

Processing

- Who immediately knew what one of the sentences was?
- Was there any miscommunication?
- How effective were you at sending your messages to the facilitator?
- What would have improved your communication?
- What are some pitfalls in communicating via text?
- What are some benefits of communicating via text?
- Have you personally had any particularly positive or negative experiences when trying to communicate via text?
- How can you avoid misunderstandings when texting is the primary avenue of communication?
- What are some messages that might be best conveyed via text message?
- What are some messages that might not be best conveyed via text message?

Go Wireless!

This activity is somewhat similar to the telephone game, in which a sentence is whispered into one person's ear, then into the next person's ear, and so on, as the group tries to pass the message around the circle in its correct form. Inevitably, errors are made and the message is muddled. Thus you can go wireless for this activity by playing the telephone game and then discussing pitfalls and benefits associated with different types of communication.

Upgrade

The recommended upgrade for this activity also qualifies as a wireless adaptation. Rather than having groups use their cell phones to discover what the sentences mean, provide each group with a printed replica of a phone keypad, then ask the teams to untangle the mixed-up sentences using only the printed information. The challenge is that participants must work to predict the text in their heads, since of course the paper keypad won't do it for them. For example, when participants are handed the message, "Jets in um vie mother!" they will have to examine the letters on the keypad in order to determine the correct phrase ("Let's go to the movies!"). When a team has the correct answer, its members can simply raise their hands and call it out.

Jets in um vie mother!

Answer: Let's go to the movies!

Yin zoo tie hand?

Answer: Who won the game?

Bam pie sick of us?

Answer: Can she pick me up?

Fo wov plax robber?

Answer: Do you play soccer?

No ox wax.

Answer: On my way.

Red walk ho dive oho

Answer: See y'all in five min

Iny zap tie done?

Answer: How was the food?

R U cycle?

Answer: Are you awake?

Tie hand zap jazz

Answer: The game was lame

Tie mother zap book!

Answer: The movie was cool!

Figure 4.3   Ten sample predictive text messages.

iSpy

Overview

It is a common lament among educators that students forget the material as soon as they leave the classroom—that there is no carryover or ability to incorporate what they have learned into their lives outside of the classroom. The iSpy activity asks participants to spend time observing other people for specific behaviors and actions that have been previously discussed in your group, then use Twitter to tweet their findings. Thus participants not only carefully observe the world around them but also dig deeper into material that is already important to your group.

Directions

This activity involves group discussion over a period of time (e.g., a week). You should purposefully choose the subject to be discussed; for example, if you are leading a group study on good listening practices, you might challenge participants to tweet when they observe someone exemplifying a characteristic of good listening. The tweet should specify what action was seen and which characteristic it exemplified. You should give the group a hashtag (e.g., #TeambuildClass101). Here is an example of an appropriate tweet:

Tweeting when one sees active listening can help participants become more aware of their own listening practices.

iSpy *(continued)*

SurferDude10 I noticed my friend being an "active listener" by nodding his head when I spoke to him about a subject. #TeambuildClass101

You might also want to challenge participants to tweet when they recognize that someone is *not* practicing good listening; if you like, you can ask participants to distinguish this type of tweet by a symbol such as a typographically rendered sad face. For example:

SurferDude10 :(When I asked my professor a question after class, she never made eye contact with me during our brief discussion. #TeambuildClass101

Group members should tweet each time they see a relevant behavior. Then, when the group meets for its next meeting, open the Web site twitter.com, project all of the tweets onto a screen via an LCD projector, and invite group members to review and discuss their tweets. One great way to initiate discussion is to give participants an opportunity to explain their tweets.

Focus
Observation: Oftentimes when a group discusses an issue, some participants feel that they learned something from the discussion; unfortunately, they often forget the lesson as soon as they leave the room. This activity helps group members apply information learned in a group setting (e.g., a classroom) as they seek examples outside of the location where they learned the material. The activity offers a great way for group members to remain connected to one another outside of regular meetings and share examples of what they have learned.

Equipment
Access to Twitter for each participant via Internet or cell phone, computer with Internet access, LCD projector

Users
10 to 20

Processing
- Share about the observations you made.
- Which characteristic was the easiest to observe?
- Were you surprised at how easy or difficult it was to find targeted characteristics displayed by others?
- Why is this characteristic important when working with a team?
- Did this assignment make you more aware of the relevance of our subject matter? How?

- Do you think awareness aids growth? (For example, does being aware of people who display characteristics of good listening make you more aware of your own listening practices?)

Go Wireless!

Rather than having participants tweet their observations, ask them to write brief descriptions of instances in which they have observed the targeted behavior. This version of the activity could also be used for anyone who does not have or does not wish to create a Twitter account. The remainder of the instructions remain the same as for the original version.

Upgrade

Rather than having participants observe strangers, ask them to watch for the targeted behaviors in their fellow group members. This approach increases the observation of your group members and reinforces the lessons that were taught during your group. For example, if you had been teaching about the characteristics of servant leadership and the group knew that they were supposed to catch each other demonstrating (or not demonstrating) these characteristics, that should lead to group members being more cognizant of the lessons taught. Likewise, when told that they should catch one another, it should lead participants to become more attentive and observant of one another. In both of these cases, the information presented (in this example, characteristics of servant leadership) is forefront in your participants' minds even outside of the teaching environment. This upgrade works best if your group members are likely to interact with one another on a regular basis outside of your formal meeting.

Tweelings

Overview

This activity uses Twitter to allow group members to share thoughts and feelings in black-and-white terminology (i.e., love versus hate). The activity gives participants a safe environment in which to offer their opinions about current events and topics of particular importance to the group. By presenting their thoughts via Twitter, group members use the technology they are comfortable with as they learn how different group members feel about the topics presented and thus develop greater understanding of one another.

Tweelings *(continued)*

Directions

Prior to the session, establish a list of subjects that can evoke strong emotions (e.g., religion, politics, the nature of the United States, immigration, sexuality, family, abortion).

To begin the activity, have participants access their Twitter account, then explain to the group that you will introduce a series of subjects about which each participant can express what he or she loves or hates about the provided subject. Each participant can give as many responses as he or she wishes. If participants use the direct messge feature, then no hashtag is needed; if they reply to the original tweet, then you do need to establish a #hashtag (see the introductory section of this chapter on p. 118 for instructions on using hashtags). Here is an example of what a question would look like on Twitter:

DrWolfeClass3940 What do you love or hate about religion?

Introduce one question at a time and have the participants tweet on the subject. The amount of tweeting time allowed is up to you, but we recommend moving to the next question when the rate of tweeting slows.

Tweeting one's opinion about various subjects creates an opportunity for group members to develop a better understanding of one another.

Give participants a 30-second warning before moving to the next question or pausing for discussion of the question just addressed. Along the way, encourage participants to tweet not only about the original question but also about tweets from others in the group.

You can either use the processing questions after each love/hate question or save the processing phase until after all questions have been discussed via tweeting. Participants also have a choice—whether to identify themselves or to remain anonymous. If a participant wishes to remain anonymous, he or she should choose a Twitter user name that does not reveal his or her identity.

Focus

Group awareness: The words *love* and *hate* are used, of course, to communicate very distinct opinions about something or someone. For most of us, some subjects in our lives or in the world evoke strong feelings, and being aware of our fellow group members' passions and dislikes helps us to negotiate effectively with each other when collaborating on various group tasks and to talk constructively about sensitive subjects.

Equipment

Access to Twitter for each participant via Internet or cell phone, computer with Internet access, LCD projector

Users

10 to 20

Processing

- Which subjects evoked the strongest emotions or opinions? Why?
- Were you surprised at some of the responses? If so, which ones, and why?
- Which subjects evoked the most negative emotions or opinions? Why? Were you surprised by this? Why or why not?
- If you remained anonymous during the activity: Do you think you would have been less likely to express some of your feelings if everyone had known your identity?
- What does this exercise tell you about working with this group?
- How can particularly strong emotions or opinions hinder a group?
- How can knowing group members' emotions and opinions help your group?

Tweelings *(continued)*

Go Wireless!

Write each subject at the top of a separate piece of blank paper, then draw a line down the center of the page to create two columns. Write *Love* at the top of one column and *Hate* at the top of the other and place the papers around the room. To promote anonymity, we recommend that you might make more than one page per subject. Having multiple pages for each subject will allow people to respond to the same topics at the same time. Additionally, participants will not know what topics people are responding to unless they are standing and waiting for an open piece of paper; however, having multiple sheets of paper will reduce this issue. Give participants an opportunity to walk around the room and write a response on either the love side or the hate side (or both, if they wish) for the different topics. When the participants are finished writing, post the pages around the room and allow participants to read the responses. Use the discussion questions provided for the original version of the activity.

Upgrade

Post the questions over a period of time (e.g., a week) by using a hashtag such as #love/hate3940. Collect the responses and discuss them during the next meeting. Here is an example of what a question and response would look like on Twitter:

DrWolfeClass3940 What do you love or hate about religion?
#love/hate3940 divisions that it causes between people.

Based on North American Mission Board, Love - Hate Outreach.

Twoogle

Overview

This activity connects your group to the world through researched presentations given by your participants and through participants' tweets that share their thoughts about how particular issues affect them. Groups are likely to grow and flourish when they have a vision larger than themselves and feel that they have a purpose and a calling. This activity offers a unique method for considering global issues and challenges your group members to see how they are affected by those issues. The upgrade for this activity asks group members to take action on a global issue.

Directions

Have participants form groups of three or four members each, then assign each group a different subject. For example, if you have three small groups, you might assign the following subjects: world hunger, AIDS in Africa, and the clean water crisis. Each group then creates a presentation on its given subject to present to the larger group. During the week, each group will provide two or three links to articles about their given subject (make sure to include an appropriate hashtag). For example, group members in the world hunger group would use their Twitter accounts to post links to articles related to world hunger. All participants should read the articles posted by the other groups. After reading the articles, individuals should tweet their responses to the following prompts:

- How does this topic affect me?
- How does this topic affect our group?

When the large group reconvenes at the end of the week (or whatever time period was designated), ask each group to share its presentation. The presentations can be as in-depth as needed and in any case should offer good general coverage of the topic. At the end of each presentation, the group's members should present the tweets made in response to the prompts for their particular topic. All group members should be encouraged to explain their tweets and offer any additional thoughts about the topic at hand.

Focus

Awareness and interconnections: With so much technology at our fingertips, we are increasingly able to be aware of global issues; we do not, however, always choose to do so, and many young people do not use technology to explore or understand issues of global concern. In many cases, their reasoning is something along the lines of "It doesn't affect me." Yet being aware of global issues and connecting them to your group are powerful ways for your group members to see how they are connected to the world around them.

Equipment

Access to Twitter for each participant via Internet or cell phone, computer with Internet access, LCD projector

Users

Groups of 3 or 4

Twoogle (*continued*)

Processing

- How does this subject affect you?
- How does this subject affect your group?
- What can you do about it?
- What will you do about it?

Go Wireless!

The wireless version of this activity eliminates the reliance on technology (including the use of Twitter) during the session, but technology is still required for researching the topic. Following the guidelines for the original version, ask each group to research a topic (provided by you) of global concern. Give the groups sufficient time to prepare their presentations, then have everyone reconvene to share their presentations with each other. Group presentations should provide an overview of the issue, and group members should pose the question prompts from the original version of the activity to the rest of the larger group's members.

Upgrade

Once each group has completed its presentation and the questions have been answered, challenge your larger group to identify one of the global issues in which group members will become actively involved, then work together as a group to develop a plan for taking action on the issue. For example, rather than just researching and talking about world hunger, your group might elect to provide money for food and clothing for a particular child living in poverty.

Following the Leader

Overview

This challenging activity uses Twitter to teach lessons about leading and following. All Twitter accounts have followers, and in 2009 there was even a competition between Ashton Kutcher and CNN to see who could attract a million followers first (it was a close race, but Kutcher won). With so many people willing to follow, it is important to consider what makes someone worth following. Likewise, what makes a good leader? This activity allows participants to explore these questions by creating their own base of followers.

Directions

Have participants form groups of three or four members each, then challenge each group to create a Twitter account and build a following. The winner is whichever group has attracted the most followers to its account at the end of a given period of time (e.g., a week). Do not give any more direction than this. Allow each group's members to brainstorm and negotiate what type of account they want to create in order to get the most followers. When the group reconvenes at the end of the given time period, have each group show their Twitter page, how many followers they have, and any interesting tweets.

Focus

Leading and following: Every group has leaders and followers, but rarely do groups stop to consider what makes a good leader, what makes a good follower, or why people lead or follow. This activity allows your group to talk about what makes people follow and lead and to explore the quality of different rationales for following and leading.

Equipment

Access to Twitter for each participant via Internet or cell phone, computer with Internet access, LCD projector

Users

Groups of 3 or 4

Creating a Twitter profile for the purpose of gathering as many followers as possible encourages groups to explore the qualities of leaders and followers.

Courtesy of Jay Keywood

Following the Leader (continued)

Processing

- What was your Twitter account name?
- How did you create your account name?
- Why did you choose this approach?
- How many followers did you have?
- How did you attract followers?
- Which group's strategy worked best? Why?
- Why do people lead?
- Why do people follow leaders?
- What makes someone a good leader or follower?
- How can you become a good leader or follower?

Go Wireless!

Tell participants that their challenge is to get as many people to follow them as they can. The idea is for people to walk around the room and convince other group members to line up behind them. Thus everyone competes for the same pool of potential followers, but once a person has decided to follow a leader, he or she cannot be stolen away; however, a leader (the person at the head of a line) can convince another leader to become a follower. In such an instance, all of that leader's followers must follow him or her to the new leader. Followers may also try to convince undecideds to join their leader. A person is identified as a follower once he or she stands behind a person that he or she has agreed to follow. As the activity progresses, the number of people trying to get followers shrinks, and the lines get longer. The activity is finished when either there is only one line left or when there are several lines whose leaders adamantly refuse to join with another group. At the completion of the activity, address the processing questions provided for the original version.

Upgrade

To increase the difficulty of this activity and to create another avenue for meaning and discussion, have groups create a Twitter profile for a not-for-profit organization that is meaningful to them instead of creating a profile for the group. As with the above directions, the challenge is still to get as many followers as possible; however, with this upgrade, the small groups would be attempting to get followers for their not-for-profit organization. In addition to providing an experience for your group, the small groups will also provide a service to selected not-for-profits. We recommend contacting the not-for-profit organizations before creating the Twitter profile so that they are aware of the task and in agreement with the method of advertisement.

5

Audio and Video Activities

This chapter explores two methods of communication and interaction that have exploded with the rapid development of new
technology: audio and video. Whether you are strolling across a
college campus or just walking down the street, the number of people
using headphones or earbuds is staggering. Music holds tremendous
importance for young people, and today's youth constantly seek out new
music. In addition, varied music is more accessible than ever before.
No longer do people have to go to a record store to purchase music;
they simply log on and download whatever they like, and this ease of
access has helped create a generation that often seems to live for music.
You will quickly see evidence of this dimension of young people's lives
as you progress through the audio activities presented in this chapter.
Your participants are likely to be both knowledgeable and passionate
about their music!

This chapter also presents activities that focus on video. It used to be
that videos were something your parents rented at the video store for the
weekend—and that they always featured highly paid Hollywood actors.
All that has changed with the rise of the Internet and various video
recording devices. Videos can now be taken via cell phone, uploaded to
a Web site (e.g., YouTube, Facebook, MySpace), and viewed by millions
of people around the world. YouTube makes virtual unknowns into

worldwide stars overnight. To see the power of videos posted via the World Wide Web, one need only look at Kimbo Slice, a street fighter whose videos were posted on YouTube and seen by executives at CBS, whereupon he (briefly) became the star of the mixed martial arts television program *Saturday Night Fights* in fall 2008, or at Susan Boyle, a 48-year-old Scottish woman who became an Internet sensation with her vocal performance of "I Dreamed a Dream" on the television show *Britain's Got Talent* in spring 2009.

This chapter presents activities that use both of these now-commonplace yet amazing media forms to teach lessons that help groups improve their teamwork and stimulate their development as high-functioning units. Activities focus on self-expression, teamwork, problem solving, comfort zones, group roles, cultural sensitivity, group consensus, stereotypes, and respect for different paths. All of the activities presented here help your group members engage with one another, develop deeper connections, and become a more cohesive and unified team.

We have addressed audio and video activities together in one chapter because they are so interwoven in the lives of today's young people. Whether watching music videos on their iPods or computers or viewing the latest YouTube sensation or viral video, they are in constant contact with both audio and video stimuli; indeed, audio and video have become almost inseparable in today's technology.

The activities presented in this chapter require the following kinds of technology: MP3 players, stereo cables, portable speakers, laptop or desktop computers, camcorders (or other video recording devices), and LCD projectors. For the audio activities, be prepared for participants to bring different types of MP3 players; you will need to have the capability to connect them to a laptop computer (preferably) or to a set of portable speakers. We recommend using a 3.5 mm [millimeter] stereo audio cable, which will connect most MP3 players to a computer via the output jack on the MP3 player and the headphone jack on the laptop or desktop computer; for iPods, we recommend using a USB charging/sync cable. And just to cover all the bases for the MP3 players that utilize special connectors or cables, we also suggest that you ask group members to bring their cables with them to the sessions where you will be using MP3 players.

In many cases, the speakers in a laptop computer create sufficient volume for all participants to hear the music, but when you have a particularly large group (more than 50), we recommend using portable speakers. None of the audio activities presented here call for you to project images onto a screen, so a laptop computer and projector are not necessary and portable speakers would be sufficient; however, a laptop computer offers more flexibility for inputs (e.g., USB cables) than portable speakers do. For example, some MP3 players may need to connect via USB or other specialized cable (that came with the MP3 player), and that is done more easily through a laptop or desktop computer. Thus the optimal set-up is to attach the MP3 player to a laptop computer that is connected to portable speakers.

For the video activities, each group must have the capability to record video (via camcorder, digital camera, or cell phone), and you must be able to project the videos onto a screen. We recommend using camcorders for On-Street Reporter, Everyone's a Critic, and First Impressions, because digital cameras and cell phones have limited recording capacity (only 30 to 60 seconds, in many cases), whereas these activities require longer video clips. For the Y3W activity, however, videos can be taken with digital cameras or cell phones. For any of the activities, once groups have collected their videos, you will need to download them to a computer. For most camcorders, you can do so via a standard USB or FireWire cable; for advanced users, some camcorders can be connected directly to an LCD projector by means of the cables that come with the camcorder, but we recommend downloading the videos to your computer because this allows for easier manipulation and editing of the files. Once you have downloaded the videos, you will be able to project them through the LCD projector, and audio can be heard through the laptop speakers or the attached portable speakers.

The All Roads Lead to Here activity requires *you* to create a video, and you can be as creative as you would like to be (and possibly enlist someone to help) as you prepare your video. We recommend using a camcorder, downloading the video to your computer as described in the preceding paragraph, and then editing your video as necessary using the free software that accompanied your computer—Windows Movie Maker for Windows users, iMovie for Mac users. In both cases, the free software is easy to use and allows you to save your videos in relatively small file sizes. Once you have edited your video as you wish, save it and download it onto USB flash drives (one for each group). Each group can then plug a USB drive into a computer and view your video about the task that its members are to complete.

This chapter contains the following activities:

- Ringtone Relay (p. 159)
- Y3W (p. 161)
- Got a Song for It! (p. 163)
- Musical Expressions (p. 166)
- What's on Your Playlist? (p. 167)
- Name That Tune (p. 170)
- On-Street Reporter (p. 172)
- Everyone's a Critic (p. 175)
- First Impressions (p. 177)
- All Roads Lead to Here (p. 180)

Setting Up a YouTube Private Group

For each of the video activities, you have the option to upload your videos to a video-sharing site such as YouTube. To create a private group on YouTube, follow these steps:

1. Visit www.youtube.com and create an account if you do not have one.
2. Roll the cursor over your user name (it will be highlighted in the upper right-hand corner).
3. Select "More" from the drop-down menu.
4. Click "Groups" from the list on the right-hand side of the page.
5. Click "Create a Group" from the list on the left-hand side of the page.
6. Complete the provided form and make sure to click the radio button for "Private."
7. Click "Invite Friends" from the list on the right-hand side of the page.
8. Invite your group members.

Ringtone Relay

Overview

Ringtones are one of the most popular high-tech means of self-expression today, and this activity uses ringtones as a springboard into a conversation about how and why people express themselves in the ways they do. Groups whose members understand how and why their fellow members express themselves have the potential to grow closer and more accepting of one another.

Directions

Prior to the activity, create a list of at least 10 types of ringtones. Possible categories include pop music, boy band music, country music, holiday music, bits of TV or movie dialogue, classical music, college fight songs, love songs, TV or movie theme music, and cartoon character voices. Some participants may also have

Challenging groups to find and share various genres of ringtones from personal cell phones helps participants learn more about one another.

designated specific ringtones to indicate calls from mom or dad, a significant other, a person they're not excited to talk to, or an ex-boyfriend or ex-girlfriend.

For the activity itself, have participants form teams of about 10 members each, then ask all participants to make sure that their cell phones are turned on. Next, tell them that you are going to call out a category of ringtone. If they have this style of ringtone in their phone, they have to find it, hold up their phone, and play the appropriate ringtone (or music) for everyone. The first two people to play the correct ringtone (or music) each get 1 point for their group. In the end, the group with the most points wins, but please remember that points are a secondary concern during this activity; most participants simply enjoy the opportunity to use their cell phones and share their music with others.

Ringtone Relay *(continued)*

Focus
Self-expression: Deep down, we all desire to be known, and it's often the case that the best activities allow people to express part of themselves in a fun and unthreatening way. This activity merges the self-expression that today's students enjoy and the technology that they thrive on. As members of your group seize the opportunity to express themselves (and as they become more comfortable with expressing themselves around their teammates), the group is likely to become more cohesive because members will understand and accept each other more fully.

Equipment
Cell phones with ringtones or music

Users
3 to 10 groups of 6 to 10

Processing
- Whose ringtone surprised you the most?
- What is the most embarrassing ringtone on your phone?
- What ringtone did you hear today that you want to get for your phone?
- What does someone's ringtone say about him or her?
- What does your ringtone say about you?
- Have you ever been embarrassed by your ringtone? When?
- Are you thinking about changing your ringtone after this activity? Why or why not?

Go Wireless!
Rather than having participants play their ringtones, ask them simply to share about songs that fit the selected categories. In this version, participants do not try to be the first to play a sample from a selected genre but simply identify as many songs as they can that fit the genre.

Upgrade
Rather than indicating certain music genres, select specific songs for participants to find on their cell phones (this approach greatly increases the difficulty of the activity). For this upgrade to be effective, it will be important to have an understanding of your group members and have an idea of the music that is on their phone. It is best to utilize this upgrade after you have played Name That Tune, Musical Expressions, Got a Song For It!, or What's on Your Playlist? because these activities give insight into the music that is on participants' MP3 players and cell phones.

Y3W

Overview

Good Morning America has a segment called Your Week in Three Words (thus the activity name) that invites viewers to submit silent videos featuring three words as a response to a particular prompt (for example, "describe your past week"). This activity works the same way, and the challenge for participants is twofold. First, it is not easy to boil one's thoughts or feelings down to a three-word response. Second, sharing one's thoughts and feelings in only three words greatly reduces one's ability to be gentle or "soften the blow," which can lead to a feeling of vulnerability (e.g., I may offend someone because I can't fully explain what I mean). At the same time, it is a powerful thing for the members of a group to accept each other's three words of self-expression, and doing so can help them create a group that is more close-knit.

Directions

Prior to your session, set up a private group on a video-sharing site such as YouTube. Ask the participants to take a picture of their three words to your chosen prompt (e.g., find their three words on signs, draw their words, write their words on their hands or arms and have someone take a picture of them, write their words on a mirror); the more creative the depiction, the better. We recommend phrasing the prompt like this: "Describe in three words [whatever you as facilitator choose for a focus]." Sample topics include the following: your year, your favorite person, your feelings about this group, your first love, your significant other, your hope for this world, your greatest dream, how you feel right now, what you want to be when you grow up, your greatest achievement, an exciting moment in your life, your response to a current situation. It may be helpful to show your participants a video example of *Good Morning America's* Y3W feature in order to give them an idea of how to approach the activity (you can easily find clips on YouTube).

Once participants have taken pictures of their three words (one picture for each word or one picture for all three words—either way is suitable), have them e-mail their images to you. When you have received all of the images, you will want to create a video. This can be done in several ways. First, you can use the free video software that comes with your computer (Windows Movie Maker for PCs and iMovie for Macs). Second, you can use higher-end software such as Final Cut or Adobe Premier. Finally, you could create a "faux-video" using PowerPoint. This is probably the least time-intensive and easiest option. Simply create slides for each of your images, select an appropriate song to play in the background, and set

Y3W *(continued)*

the slides to advance automatically after approximately 5 seconds. When viewed in presentation mode, this will give the appearance of a video. At the session itself, have the group view the video that includes all of their three words and discuss the results.

Focus

Acceptance and self-expression: This activity requires individuals to express themselves in a creative manner, which can be a daunting task for some group members if they feel unsure of how others will react. Thus it is vital that you work to create an atmosphere of trust and acceptance in which participants feel comfortable expressing their answers. An atmosphere of openness, along with participants' willingness to share, can draw your group of individuals closer to one another and create a more close-knit team.

Equipment

Access to a digital recording device for each person (e.g., Webcam, cell phone, digital camera, camcorder), Internet connection, computer, LCD projector

Users

10 to 20

Processing

Begin the processing by asking each person the same question: Why those three words?

- Where you surprised by anyone's three words?
- Which three words did you find most interesting? Why?
- Was it hard for you to come up with just three words? Why or why not?
- How would this exercise have been different if you had been asked to share verbally?
- How would this exercise be different if you had to prepare your three words for strangers?
- Why is a three-word response powerful (or not powerful)?
- What did you learn about acceptance and self-expression from this activity?

Go Wireless!

Instead of having participants use photos, simply ask each person during the session to spend a moment thinking of three words that would describe his or her feelings in response to a particular prompt. Participants can either write down their words or simply remember them and share them with the group when their turn comes.

Upgrade

Rather than have participants capture their three words with still pictures, ask them to creatively capture their words on video. The prompts will remain the same; however, the way the responses are depicted will significantly change. Each person then shows his or her video to the group. Another variation of this version of the activity is for the facilitator to combine all of the three-word videos into one large video montage. If you are an amateur (or professional) videophile, you can create a particularly powerful montage through the use of striking transitions and animations.

Got a Song for It!

Overview

Problem solving and teamwork are two of the most common topics explored during team-building sessions, and this activity challenges participants to work together in using their MP3 players to identify and play songs that include certain words. As they brainstorm together, participants will find opportunities to connect in ways that bring them closer to one another. Even though not all participants will have a matching song for every prompt, all members are still actively involved as they work together to think of songs that others might have stored on their players. As group members work together to identify song titles, they will have opportunities to experience and explore different roles (e.g., some group members will have lots of songs on their MP3 players, while other group

Participants work together to find song titles and play songs from their MP3 players with certain words in them.

members may not have as many songs on theirs but know more songs that fit the category). It is when group members understand and embrace their specific roles that groups have the ability to truly develop and grow.

Got a Song for It! *(continued)*

Directions

Prior to the session, compose a list of 5 to 10 key words; see suggestions below.

Sample words to use:

- Love
- Hate
- Rain
- Hot
- Cold
- Boy
- Girl
- Dance
- Cry
- Promise
- Grass
- Police
- Fight
- Kiss
- Play
- Baby
- Light
- Night
- Broke
- Summer
- Fall
- Winter
- Spring
- Time
- America

Start the session by having participants form teams of three or four members each, then state or show (via presentation software such as PowerPoint) the first word on your list and instruct the teams to find and play a song that includes the word from a team member's MP3 player. The first group to play an appropriate song receives 1 point. The song does not have to be played in its entirety or until the words are heard; trust the group members that the song contains the correct lyrics. You can award half of a point to a team that identifies a correct song but does not have it stored on an MP3 player. The teams battle back and forth until all of the selected (5 to 10) key words have been used.

Note: Points should be only a secondary concern in doing this activity; the real purpose is not to win but to focus on teamwork, problem solving, and participant roles.

Focus

Teamwork and problem solving: Throughout life, we are called on to serve in groups in order to solve difficult problems. As a result, it is a particularly valuable life skill for anyone to learn how to function as an effective and contributing member of a team, and this activity allows participants to gain experience both in working as part of a team and working to solve a problem. Some members of the team may have more songs and thus be able to contribute more to the group during this particular activity, but all members will be able to help by thinking of appropriate songs. Thus, if a group is to succeed in this activity, its members must work together.

Equipment

Personal MP3 players or cell phones

Users

Groups of 3 or 4

Processing

- Which word was the easiest to match with a song?
- Were any words impossible to match?
- What process did your team use to identify appropriate songs?
- How did your team work together during the activity?
- What was the most difficult part of the task?
- What groups, other than this one, are you part of?
- What are some of the problems that one of your other groups has to solve?
- How have you attempted to solve problems in that group?
- How could your large group work together to solve problems more effectively?

Go Wireless!

Instead of having teams play appropriate songs from their MP3 players, have them identify songs (by name) that contain the specified word. For additional fun, you could ask the group or person who identified the song to sing the line that includes the specified lyric.

Upgrade

Have the group identify songs (either by name or by playing them from an MP3 player) in categories that are meaningful to the group. For example, if the group is learning about servant leadership, teams could be asked to identify songs that refer to leadership or service work. Other possible topics include disability, politics, and current events.

Musical Expressions

Overview

Not everyone is comfortable expressing himself or herself in the same ways, and some forms of self-expression can be very uncomfortable to certain people. This activity asks each participant to stand in front of the group and act out a particular song, which may be quite challenging for some group members, but being able to identify and expand one's comfort zone is a valuable skill to develop. The processing phase of this activity challenges participants to explore the nature of comfort zones and how they can both hinder and further a group's growth and development.

Directions

Have participants form teams of four or five members each and ask each team to select three of its members' favorite songs from their MP3 players. Each group should write its chosen song titles down (on individual index cards) and give the cards to the facilitator, who should then mix all of the cards in a hat and select one team to begin the activity.

Next, each team should identify one member to serve as its musician, another as its actor, and a third as its artist. The group's musician selects a card with a song title from the hat and has 30 seconds to hum enough of the song for the rest of the team to identify it. If the team does not guess the song within 30 seconds, the actor stands up and acts out the song (without using words or any vocalizations) for 30 seconds. If the team still does not guess the song, the artist gets 30 seconds to draw the title of the song (again, without using any words). If the team cannot guess the song title after the full 90 seconds, any other team may have one attempt to name the song title. Proceed in this fashion until all of the titles in the hat have been used.

Focus

Comfort zone: Everyone has a comfort zone—a physical, social, or emotional place where he or she feels most comfortable. The problem with most comfort zones is that they may not overlap with other individuals' comfort zones; as a result, they can limit us in meeting or interacting with other types of people. This activity pushes people outside of their comfort zones, and therefore you should approach it with care, since some individuals may feel considerably anxious about humming, acting, or drawing in front of the group. However, in order for a group to grow, group members must learn to create a safe environment where people feel comfortable, and since this activity calls on participants to express themselves in a way that may be slightly uncomfortable, it gives them a chance to stretch their comfort zones so that they can feel more at ease about working with and around one another. You should make this purpose of the activity crystal clear from the beginning, and participants should be allowed to sit it out if they so desire.

Equipment

Individual MP3 players, index cards, writing utensils, large pads of paper for drawing

Users

Groups of 4 or 5

Processing

- Which role did you choose to play? Why?
- Were you ever out of your comfort zone during this activity? When?
- Describe your typical comfort zones in your daily life.
- What are the advantages of comfort zones?
- What are the disadvantages of comfort zones?
- How can we minimize the disadvantages and maximize the advantages of comfort zones?

Go Wireless!

Rather than searching their MP3 players for song ideas, participants can simply think about their favorite songs and create a top three list for the group.

Upgrade

Play multiple rounds of the game and ask that participants take on a different role in each round. This approach maximizes the chance that all participants will spend at least some time outside of their comfort zone and thus have a personal experience to share during the processing stage.

What's on Your Playlist?

Overview

This activity provides opportunities for self-expression as group members try to identify songs from one another's MP3 players. To avoid potential conflicts within a group, it is important that group members understand how their fellow members express themselves. A given person's method of

What's on Your Playlist? *(continued)*

self-expression may catch someone off guard or make others feel uncomfortable, and it is a necessary step in the group's growth for members to accept how other people choose to express themselves and recognize how their own self-expression may affect others. For example, some people react very loudly and vociferously to either good or bad news, whereas others accept news stoically, and honoring these different styles of self-expression helps group members grow closer to one another.

Directions

Prior to the activity, collect MP3 players (or cell phones) from the participants. (All participants do not need to give up their phones, but the more who do, the better.) When you begin the session, play some preselected songs from the "recently played" list or "recently downloaded" list on each MP3 player or cell phone. (We recommend that you practice with each of the devices before starting so that you can maneuver your way through each device with ease.) After you have played enough of a song for participants to identify it, ask them if they can identify who in the group would have that particular song on his or her MP3 player or cell phone; play three songs before asking the group for its final answer. Then have the owner identify himself or herself. Continue this process until all MP3 players or cell phones have been used.

Group members express themselves by sharing music from their personal playlists.

Focus

Self-expression: People choose to express themselves in a multitude of ways. Some express themselves in the clothes they wear, while others do so in the music they listen to. In fact, music not only helps some people define who they are; it can also inspire, and this activity allows participants to give fellow group members a glimpse into their lives and initiate a conversation about self-expression and inspiration through music.

Equipment

Personal MP3 players or cell phones, computer with speakers for MP3 players that do not have external speakers, cables with which to attach MP3 players to computer

Users

10 to 20

Processing

- What was your favorite song of those you heard?
- Which song will you download later?
- Which person's music most surprised you?
- What can you learn about a person from his or her music?
- What does music do for us? Why do we listen to it?
- What are some examples of inspirational songs?
- Can music inspire people to complete negative acts? What examples can you cite?
- How can we learn to motivate others by understanding the music that motivates them?

Go Wireless!

Rather than playing music from participants' MP3 players or cell phones, have them form teams of three or four members each and have each team create a list of 10 favorite songs. Then give each team a chance to share its list with the rest of the group and have the group's members explain why they chose the songs they did.

Upgrade

To increase the activity's effectiveness, ask group members to load their favorite music onto their MP3 player or cell phone before the session. Then, during the session, have each person play his or her three favorite songs; once the group has heard all three songs, the person who chose them can explain the significance that each song holds for him or her.

Name That Tune

Overview

This activity uses music from participants' MP3 players to help them see how well they know one another and how well they know various kinds of music. Participants are asked to guess song titles, which may prove difficult for some individuals; however, as with the Trivia Text activity (p. 135), Name That Tune highlights the strengths of various participants and enables you to discuss the nature of individual roles within a group. Some people will know all the songs, others will know none of them, and still others will be able to offer ideas but not exact titles. The intent is for your group to enter into (or continue) a discussion about roles and about the importance of having everyone play and embrace a role within the group.

Directions

Ask participants to bring their MP3 players with them to the session. Begin the session by having participants form teams of three or four members each, then collect all the MP3 players (keep each team's MP3 players together). Select one team to begin the activity, then pick one song from the "most played" or "recently played" list of one of the team's MP3 players. Connect the MP3 player to speakers and play the first 5 seconds of the song. As soon as the music ends, any team (except the team from which the MP3 player came) can attempt to guess the name of the song. If a team identifies the song title (or comes close), award that team 1 point and move on to the next team's MP3 player. If no team is able to identify the song, play it for 30 seconds or until a team correctly offers the title (whichever comes first). Award 1 point to a team that first guesses the song title (or comes close to it) within this interval. If no one guesses correctly after 30 seconds, state the name of the song and move on to the next team's MP3 players. Continue this process for 10 to 15 different songs.

Winning points is only a secondary concern during this activity; the true purpose is not to win the most points but to discover and become comfortable with participant roles within the group.

Focus

Group roles: This activity requires teams to listen carefully in order to identify songs, and participants often find themselves either knowing all of the answers or knowing none of them. The activity may be particularly enjoyable for those who know all (or many) of the answers, whereas those who know few if any answers may find themselves frustrated and bored. Participants in either camp should be given a chance to share their thoughts and feelings at the end of the activity. The intent is for individuals to begin to identify their roles within the group in the hope of becoming comfortable with those roles and recognizing that their roles may change from activity to activity. Additionally, while some individuals may not know the titles of the songs, they may still be able to participate meaningfully by virtue of having heard the songs and knowing the lyrics or simply taking part in the group discussion that leads to naming a song. While such roles may not be obvious to all participants during the activity, you can highlight them during the processing phase.

Equipment

Personal MP3 players or cell phones, computer with speakers for MP3 players that do not have external speakers, cables with which to attach MP3 players to the computer

Users

Groups of 3 or 4

Processing

- Which song was the hardest to identify? Why?
- Which song was the easiest to identify? Why?
- Who knew the most answers?
- Who knew the fewest answers?
- How would you describe your role during this activity?
- Is that the role you wanted to have, or is there another role that you would have preferred?
- How would you describe your role within this group more generally?
- Is that the role you want to have, or is there another role that you would prefer?
- How can you further develop and become comfortable with your role within this group?
- How can we help each other in this process?

Go Wireless!

The wireless option for this activity requires additional preparation. Rather than asking participants to bring their MP3 players to the session, search the Web for lyrics to current popular songs (we recommend using www.lyrics.com). When participants arrive for the session, have them form teams of three or four members each and give each team the lyrics to about five songs (each team should have a different five songs). Ask the first group to read lines from one of the selected songs and see if the other teams can identify the song; the first team to do so wins 1 point. Continue until all of the songs have been used.

Name That Tune *(continued)*

Upgrade

This upgrade also involves additional preparation. Before the session, search the Web for songs that would be particularly helpful with issues that your group is facing. For example, you might look for songs addressing loss, excitement, happiness, or sorrow. As you find appropriate songs, download them so that you can play them for the group. When participants arrive for the session, play the selected songs as indicated in the guidelines for the original version of the activity. During the processing phase, you can address your rationale for selecting each song.

On-Street Reporter

Overview

Everyone has his or her own point of view, especially in hot-button areas such as religion and politics, and this activity asks participants to grapple with such sensitive issues by interviewing strangers. This experience helps participants to understand that different people often hold different opinions and to mature in their ability to work with each other—accepting each other's opinions, or agreeing to disagree about them—during group endeavors. The processing questions for this activity challenge your group members to explore their own thoughts and feelings about the questions, about various answers, and about the people who provided those answers.

Directions

Have participants form teams of three or four members each and instruct the groups to go out and conduct video interviews with strangers on the street. They must try to interview five different people, and they may not approach anyone they already know. Each group will ask its interviewees the same question but should attempt to identify and interview people with as diverse a range of opinions as possible. The question you choose could address most anything, but your priority as facilitator should be to get a cross section of responses about a particular issue of concern to the group with which you are working. Here are some possibilities:

- Why are we here?
- Is there a God?
- Can we solve world hunger? If so, how? If not, why not?

Interviewing people outside of the group creates an opportunity for participants to grow in their understanding that people have different opinions and mature in their ability to work with others who are different from them.

- If you became president of the United States, what is the first thing you would do?
- Which is the more important issue: homelessness or lack of educational opportunity?
- When will you have enough money?
- What are three things that you will never do?
- What effect do you want to have on the world?
- What would make you happy?
- Where is your "happy place"?
- What is your proudest moment so far?
- What inspires you?
- What is your guilty pleasure?
- What scares you?

Groups should be told to ask permission before recording and to respect the wishes of those with whom they speak (or attempt to speak). Each time this activity is done, select one question prompt to be asked of all five interviewees in order to facilitate comparisons of answers and

On-Street Reporter *(continued)*

minimize the time needed for each interview. After the groups have completed their interviews, they should return to the base location for the session and upload their video to a computer. Now the whole group can watch the videos together.

Focus

Sensitivity to different viewpoints on difficult topics: The purpose of this activity is to introduce difficult topics to your group and provide a safe opportunity for discussing them. Beginning with interviews of people outside the group creates a safe starting point for such a conversation within your group, and providing this kind of safe opportunity for conversation on difficult topics allows group members to learn to understand and respect members' viewpoints that may be different from the majority within the group.

Equipment

Digital cameras or camcorders for recording videos, computer, LCD projector (Note: Facilitators should gather enough digital cameras or camcorders for each group. If the facilitator finds it difficult to do so, the activity can be done over a period of time, so that each group can check out a camera for its recordings. Participants who own such devices can also elect to use their own equipment for the activity. Cell phone video cameras will probably not be useful for this activity because their recording time is usually quite limited.)

Users

Groups of 3 or 4

Processing

Processing for this activity begins with groups sharing their videos.

- How would you answer the question?
- Which answer to the question was most like yours?
- Which answer to the question was least like yours?
- Which response made you laugh?
- Which response made you hurt?
- How did people react to the question?
- How did people react to being interviewed?
- How did you predict whether someone would give you a distinctive or unusual answer?
- Did stereotypes come into play at all?

- What did you learn about the particular issue?
- What can you do right now to find your answer to the question you posed to your interviewees?

Go Wireless!

Rather than video-record everything that people said, teams could conduct their interviews without a camera and simply write down the answers. Then, when the teams return, they could simply share the responses they heard.

Upgrade

To increase the difficulty of this task, participants could interview each of their team members before they go out to interview members of the public. Interviewing each other forces participants to experience what their interviewees are going to experience and encourages them to address the issue themselves rather than just explore how other people feel about it.

Everyone's a Critic

Overview

This activity asks your group to locate video clips that fit selected categories, and as participants work in small groups to reach consensus about which videos to share they gain understanding of the importance and the nature of consensus building. Then, when the teams share their chosen video clips with the larger group, the resulting discussions provide the foundation for a group conversation about cultural sensitivity as participants see how their selections may sometimes be offensive to others. There is a fine line between laughing with a person and laughing at that person, and groups whose members understand how to be sensitive to other groups are also more likely to be sensitive to one another.

Directions

Have participants form teams of three or four members each and give each team the use of a computer with Internet access. Each team should go to an Internet video site (e.g., YouTube) and search for videos that fit a category that you assign. Some possible categories are humor, inspiration, educational clips, animals, children, dancing, amazing feats, vehicles, and sports. Each team's goal should be to find videos that fit the category and are new to the rest of the larger group so that they retain their potential for sparking spontaneous reactions. At the same time, emphasize to the

Everyone's a Critic *(continued)*

teams that you are looking for videos that not only fit the specified category but also are not offensive to any group of people. Once each team has reached a consensus regarding its top video, ask all of the teams whether they would show their chosen clip to a younger sibling or grandparent. If they say no, ask them to explain why. After using this method to screen videos for acceptability and appropriateness, have the small groups show their videos to the larger group.

Focus

Cultural sensitivity and group consensus: What one person finds funny, fascinating, or amazing can be deeply offensive to someone else, or even to a whole group of people. Learning to be culturally sensitive takes thought and consideration, and people have to be willing to step out of their cultural cocoons and see the world through another person's eyes. This activity uses a very popular medium (Web video) to help participants explore their own ability to be culturally sensitive. It also helps participants learn to participate constructively in developing group consensus as the small teams work through the difficult process of coming to agreement on a top video for the selected category.

Equipment

Computer with Internet connection for each team, LCD projector

Users

Groups of 3 or 4

Processing

Questions for the team that selected the video:

- Why did your team choose this video?
- What was your selection process? Did everyone have a say?
- Is your video sensitive to other groups of people? How so, or how not?
- What do you want the larger group to learn from watching the video you selected?

Questions for the rest of the larger group:

- Would you show this video to others? Why or why not?
- What did you like about this video?
- What did you not like about it?
- What are some lessons that can be learned from this video?

Go Wireless!

In order to focus on cultural sensitivity, you could have participants discuss popular videos they have seen on the Web and in other places. Ask participants to list several videos they consider to be funny, fascinating, or exciting (you do not have to provide specific categories or prompts), then have the group talk about the cultural sensitivity (or lack thereof) that characterizes the suggested videos.

Upgrade

Give each team a topic about which to create its own video to post on YouTube. For example, you might ask groups to create a video to encourage environmentally sustainable or "green" practices such as recycling, or you might ask them to address world hunger or a certain cause that is personally meaningful. Each group's members can choose the tone to strike in their video (e.g., funny, inspirational, scary, educational).

First Impressions

Overview

This activity challenges participants to interview strangers and ask them several yes-or-no and "would you rather" questions, and the responses they gather create a framework within which your group can discuss the issue of stereotypes. In many cases, participants make comments such as, "I never expected someone who looked like that to say that." It is this mentality that stereotypes are founded on, and stereotypes can destroy groups. Thus, having a frank discussion related to stereotypes and how we "box people in" can improve your group members' ability to understand one another and work well together.

Directions

Have participants go out in groups of three or four members each and find approximately 10 strangers to interview. The interview question should be a simple yes-or-no or either-or inquiry. Here are a few examples:

- Did you brush your teeth this morning?
- Are you a vegetarian?
- Do you consider yourself a white-collar worker or a blue-collar worker?
- Are you a smoker?

First Impressions *(continued)*

Group members explore stereotypes by interviewing people outside the group with yes-or-no questions and guessing the response of the interviewee based on first impression.

- Are you a regular church attendee?
- Do you have a college degree?
- Do you drive a hybrid?
- Are you a Republican or Democrat?
- Do you prefer solitude or groups of people?
- Do you prefer dogs or cats?
- Do you prefer hot dogs or hamburgers?
- Would you rather lose your legs or lose your arms?
- Would you rather be 3 feet tall or 8 feet tall?
- Would you rather get even or get over it?
- Would you rather give bad advice or take it?
- Would you rather run a mile or give a public speech?

Remind participants to be respectful of their subjects and careful about the manner in which they ask for an interview. They should also have their interviewees pause prior to answering the question so that there is a brief delay between the question and the response (as you'll see, this delay will be useful to you during the activity's processing phase). Finally, make sure that teams know to allow their interviewees time to explain the rationale for their response if they so desire.

When the groups have completed their interviews, have them come back and upload their videos onto a computer. Display each group's work, but stop the video right before the interviewee gives the answer and ask the other teams if they think they know how the person will respond. Once the other teams have offered their suggestions, view the interviewee's response. Repeat this process for all of the videos.

Focus

Stereotypes: We all make judgments about other people without knowing them. We look at someone and assume, on the basis of some characteristic (e.g., gender, race, age, hair color, clothing style) that we know what that person thinks and how he or she will respond in a given situation. This activity provides an opportunity for group members to explore the importance of withholding judgment of people before getting to know them. When you ask group members to anticipate interviewees' responses to the questions, you are asking them to judge a person they don't know—something that is done all the time but is not generally helpful. Thus this activity allows participants to see some of the problems inherent in stereotypical thinking and assumptions.

Equipment

Digital cameras or camcorders for recording videos, computer, LCD projector

Users

Groups of 3 or 4

Processing

- Is there a question that *you* wanted to answer? Why?
- Which answer surprised you the most? Why?
- How often were you correct in your assumption about how a person would respond?
- What role did stereotypes play in this activity?
- Are stereotypes good or bad? Why?
- What did you learn about stereotypes?
- How can you use what you have learned about stereotypes in your dealings with people?

Go Wireless!

Teams can conduct their interviews without a camera and simply write down the answers to their question. Then, when the teams return, rather than watching videos, they simply share the responses they gathered.

First Impressions *(continued)*

Upgrade

Have participants interview other members of their small group, then proceed with the instructions for the original version of the activity. This upgrade forms a nice contrast to the original version because in this case participants most likely make decisions about how a person will respond based on their knowledge of the person rather than on their perception of the person's appearance.

All Roads Lead to Here

Overview

We have all taken different paths to reach our current position in life. The unique fact for the particular group you are working with is that, while the journeys have all been different, they have all led to the same place—your group. This activity hinges on a metaphor that allows your group members to compare the journey they take in the activity with the journeys they have taken in life. The processing questions encourage participants to share about their journeys and discuss the different paths they have taken to reach the current group, and as they share their experiences they will find ways to grow closer to one another.

Directions

Have participants form teams of three or four members each and give each team a set of brief video instructions that lead eventually to a final location. The videos might simply show a person stating the instructions or they might be more elaborate; for example, you could use a person dressed as a certain character to communicate the directions or use editing software to make a more creative presentation. For additional suggestions related to this activity, review the Trailing the Text activity presented in chapter 4 (specifically the clues presented in figure 4.2 on p. 133).

Each team should have a different set of directions, but all teams should end at the same location; only the routes for getting there should differ from team to team. Do not, however, tell the teams that they all have the same destination, just to add to the mystery. Your video directions might lead the groups through various kinds of places. For example, on a college campus, one set of directions could take a team through an athletic complex, Greek housing, academic buildings, music buildings, and the campus theater, whereas another team might go through the same locations but in a different order. Another approach would be to direct teams to different rooms and through different hallways within the same large building to reach their final destination. On a larger scale, you might have teams navigate different city streets to reach the final place.

The video instructions should require each group to collect an object or a certain type of information at each location (this requirement prevents groups from just watching the entire video and going directly to the final location). You might choose to plant objects at each location, but it is not necessary to go that far. For example, if you send participants to a library, each group could be required to get a piece of paper with a return date stamped on it (e.g., a copy of a receipt for a checked-out book).

Once the teams have been formed, give each team a USB flash drive that contains its video instructions (you'll also need a computer on which each team can view its instructions). Teams should watch their video in its entirety because they will not have access to it once they leave the starting location. Once a team has watched the video and determined its path and the objects that must be collected, it may begin its journey. Once all groups have reached the final destination, allow them to share about the paths they traveled and the experiences they had along the way.

Focus

Different paths: We are all prone to think at times that if something isn't done our way, it isn't being done right, and this activity is designed to dispel that myth. Participants are asked to find a hidden location, but each group must take a different path to get there. The design of this activity allows you to draw a simple metaphor comparing the different paths (leading to the same destination) that participants take during the activity with the different paths that people take when completing tasks and living life. Not everyone does things in the same way. Not everyone thinks in the same way. This activity embraces the different paths that people take and allows participants to see that the fact that something wasn't done their way doesn't necessarily mean that it was done incorrectly.

Equipment

Preparing the videos requires a camcorder or other digital video recording device and a computer. Facilitators can add to the atmosphere by creating videos with dramatic action-movie or spy-movie music in the background. For each group, you will need a USB flash drive that contains a copy of the video.

Users

Groups of 3 or 4

All Roads Lead to Here *(continued)*

Processing
- What was your route?
- Where did you think you were going, and what led you to believe that?
- What was the most interesting thing you saw on your journey?
- Describe your journey.
- Why do you think each group was given a different route?
- What path have you taken to get where you are in life?
- What can we learn from the fact that although everyone has a different journey we are all in the same place right now?
- How do the different journeys taken by others help you in your journey?

Go Wireless!
Rather than creating video instructions, prepare cards with images or verbal directions for your participants.

Upgrade
There are several options for increasing the difficulty of the activity. First, you can make the directions intentionally vague; be aware, however, that leaving them too vague can make the task nearly impossible. A second option is to have the teams complete different tasks at each of the waypoints; for example, rather than simply collecting an object or information, teams could be asked to participate in a brief activity such as picking up trash. You can also upgrade the activity simply by adding more waypoints to the journey, thus increasing the amount of time required to complete the journey and giving participants more experiences to share afterward. Finally, of course, you can use a combination of these adaptations to substantially increase the challenge.

Bibliography

Allport, G.W. 1954. *The nature of prejudice*. New York: Addison-Wesley.

Bucher, K.T., and M.L. Manning. 2005. Creating safe schools. *The Clearing House* 79: 55-60.

Davis-Berman, J., and D. Berman. 2002. Risk and anxiety in adventure programming. *Journal of Experiential Education* 25: 305-310.

Devine, M.A., and J. Dattilo. 2000. Expressive arts as therapeutic media. In *Facilitation techniques in therapeutic recreation*, ed. J. Dattilo, 133-164. State College, PA: Venture Publishing.

Dewey, J. 1938. *Education and experience*. New York: Macmillan Co.

Eden Prairie students walk out in protest. 2008. Associated Press, January 10. http://minnesota.publicradio.org/display/web/2008/01/10/ephs_protest/.

Go, A. 2007. Columnist says he was fired for Facebook comments. *U.S. News & World Report*, February 27. www.usnews.com/blogs/paper-trail/2007/02/27/columnist-says-he-was-fired-for-facebook-comments/comments/.

Heerman, B. 1997. *Building team spirit: Activities for inspiring and energizing teams*. New York: McGraw-Hill.

Junco, R., and J. Mastrodicasa. 2007. *Connecting to the Net.Generation: What higher education professionals need to know about today's students*. Washington, DC: NASPA.

Kolb, D.A. 1984. *Experiential learning: Experience as the source of learning and development*. Englewood Cliffs, NJ: Prentice Hall.

Matyszczyk, C. 2009. Facebook post gets NFL Eagles' worker fired. CNET.com, March 9. http://news.cnet.com/8301-17852_3-10192227-71.html.

Prensky, M. 2005–2006. Listen to the natives. *Educational Leadership* 63 (4): 8-13.

Shapira, I. 2008. What comes next after Generation X? As a demographic, millennials don't all see it as the best label. *Washington Post*, July 6.

Siler, G. 1994. *Centrifuge games with a purpose*. Nashville, TN: Convention Press.

Tapscott, D. 2008. *Grown up digital: How the Net Generation is changing your world*. New York: McGraw-Hill.

Tripp, A., R. French, and C. Sherill. 1995. Contact theory and attitudes of children in physical education. *Adapted Physical Activity Quarterly* 12: 323-332.

Waxer, C. 2009. Clash of the generations: A twist of fate has technology vets and fresh talent vying for the same jobs. *Computerworld* (February 16): 16-20.

Zahari, E. 2008. The Flickr game. http://kamigoroshi.net/web/meme/the-flickr-game.

Additional sources for team-building activities:

Barrett, B. 2005. *Games for the whole child*. Champaign, IL: Human Kinetics.

Cain, J., and T. Smith. 2002. *The book on raccoon circles*. Tulsa, OK: Learning Unlimited.

Fluegelman, A. 1976. *The new games book*. Garden City, NY: Doubleday.

Fluegelman, A. 1981. *More new games*. Garden City, NY: Doubleday.

Hohenstein, M. 1980. *Games*. Minneapolis: Bethany Fellowship.

Luckner, J.L., and R.S. Nadler. 1997. *Processing the experience: Strategies to enhance and generalize learning*. 2nd ed. Dubuque, IA: Kendall Hunt.

Midura, D.W., and D.R. Glover. 1995. *More teambuilding challenges*. Champaign, IL: Human Kinetics.

Priest, S., and K. Rohnke. 2000. *101 of the best corporate team-building activities*. Dubuque, IA: Kendall Hunt.

Rohnke, K. 1988. *The bottomless bag*. Beverly, MA: Wilkscraft Creative Printing.

Rohnke, K. 1988. *Silver bullets*. Beverly, MA: Wilkscraft Creative Printing.

Rohnke, K., and S. Butler. 1996. *Quicksilver: Adventure games, initiative problems, trust activities and a guide to effective leadership*. Dubuque, IA: Kendall Hunt.

About the Authors

Brent D. Wolfe, PhD, is assistant professor in the department of hospitality, tourism, and family and consumer sciences at Georgia Southern University in Statesboro.

Working in higher education for the past decade, Wolfe has developed and taught courses on facilitating experiential and team-building activities. Specifically, Wolfe uses experiential activities with university freshmen to promote unity in the classroom and connectedness to the university. Working with these students allows him continued involvement with young adults and their unique interests, perspectives, and life challenges.

Wolfe has presented his research on facilitation and debriefing at numerous international and national conferences and has authored several peer-reviewed journal articles and book chapters. In 2006, he was awarded the Junior Faculty Outstanding Teaching Award from the University of Southern Mississippi.

As a certified therapeutic recreation specialist, Wolfe works as a consultant for the Luckday Citizenship Scholars Program, developing and testing new team-building techniques and practicing his group-development and relationship-building skills.

Wolfe is a member of the National Therapeutic Recreation Society where he currently serves as president. He was also a member of the Association for Challenge Course Technology and the Association for Outdoor Recreation and Education.

In his free time, Wolfe enjoys learning about the latest in digital technologies. He also enjoys playing disc golf and hide-and-seek with his two-year-old daughter. He resides in Statesboro with his wife, Rebecca, and their daughter, Austyn Grace.

Colbey Penton Sparkman has more than 10 years of experience working with young adults as a campus minister and church-based minister. Previously, she served as minister to collegiates at First Baptist Church in Hattiesburg and as a campus minister at Florida State University and the University of Louisiana at Monroe.

Penton Sparkman currently works as a leadership development consultant and communications specialist for National Collegiate Ministry. She received her master of divinity degree in 2000 from Southwestern Baptist Theological Seminary.

Penton Sparkman, her husband, Larry, and three young daughters live in Hattiesburg, Mississippi. In her leisure time she enjoys graphic design, triathlon training, and vegetable gardening.

You'll find other outstanding
recreation resources at
www.HumanKinetics.com

In the U.S. call 1.800.747.4457
Australia 08 8372 0999
Canada. 1.800.465.7301
Europe . . . . .+44 (0) 113 255 5665
New Zealand 0800 222 062

HUMAN KINETICS
The Information Leader in Physical Activity & Health
P.O. Box 5076 • Champaign, IL 61825-5076